A CUP OF COMFORT®

for

Horse Lovers

Stories that celebrate the
extraordinary relationship
between horse and rider

Edited by Colleen Sell

A **adams**media
Avon, Massachusetts

For Samantha—dear friend, gifted storyteller,
passionate horsewoman

Published by
Adams Media, an F+W Publications Company
57 Littlefield Street, Avon, MA 02322 U.S.A.
www.adamsmedia.com and www.cupofcomfort.com

ISBN 10: 1-59869-655-6
ISBN 13: 978-1-59869-655-4

Printed in the United States of America.

J I H G F E D C B A

Library of Congress Cataloging-in-Publication Data
is available from the publisher.

*This book is available at quantity discounts for bulk purchases.
For information, please call 1-800-289-0963.*

Contents

Acknowledgments

My gratitude extends to a long list of special people:

The hopeful horse lovers who submitted their personal stories for publication consideration in this book;

The talented talespinners whose personal stories grace these pages;

My collaborators at Adams Media: Meredith O'Hayre, Laura Daly, Paula Munier, Jennifer Bright Reich, Heather Barrett, and Colleen Cunningham.

My family and friends, for being my champions and my comic diversions;

And you, dear reader, for allowing us to share these exceptional stories with you.

Introduction

"The essential joy of being with horses is that it brings us in contact with the rare elements of grace, beauty, spirit, and fire."

Sharon Ralls Lemon

I've always felt a connection with horses, which might seem odd, given that I've had minimal exposure to horses—a couple of pony rides, one magnificent gallop on a distant relative's gelding, a few guided trail rides, and now, visiting neighbors' horses on my daily walks. Still, despite having only those minimal experiences with horses, I have always felt a deep connection with them. And it is more than fondness and fascination. More so, it is a soul connection. I am certainly not alone. A staggering number of horse lovers—ranging from those who merely dream of horses to those who live and breathe horses—speak of that same inexplicable, almost magical, connection with horses. It seems to be innate.

In fact, the horse-human connection goes back more than 6,000 years. For most of history, horses were the primary means of transportation and the "horse power" used to fight wars and cultivate land, playing a pivotal role in the rise and spread of civilization. For thousands of years, humans have teamed up with horses for sport and recreation. More recently, horses have been used therapeutically, to help heal human bodies, minds, and spirits. Always, our equine friends have given us companionship, comfort, pleasure, and pride.

Many people believe that the human-horse connection goes beyond the physical and emotional—to the spiritual or mystical. Most horse lovers find it difficult to believe otherwise. We are awestruck by the beauty, strength, agility, and spirit of horses. We are humbled by their intelligence, affection for us, willingness to do as we ask, and ability to "read" us. More than any other species on Earth—even "man's best friend," dogs—equines can understand our verbal and physical commands as well as intuit our emotions, body language, and intent (willful energy).

Yet, we are never the horse's "master." They "listen" to us only when, and if, we earn their allegiance, never when we try to force their submission.

Nor is a horse ever fully "tamed." No matter how well-trained and tuned-in horses are, they remain independent spirits, forces of nature. So we must learn to read them, too. Our equine partners give as they receive, and the magical partnership between horse and human is based on mutual respect, trust, communication, support, and love.

The personal essays in *A Cup of Comfort® for Horse Lovers* reveal the myriad ways in which horses connect with humans, enriching—and, in some cases, saving—the lives of both. These heartwarming true stories pay fitting tribute to one of nature's most beautiful creatures and to one of life's most beautiful relationships, affirming writer Alice Walker's assertion that "horses make a landscape"—both in nature and within the soul—"more beautiful."

Enjoy.

Colleen Sell

The Pony Farm

The kids and grandkids were home for the holidays, and the house was chaotic with noise and motion. In the midst of swirling holiday activities, I was sorting through Christmas cards and found one from someone I hadn't thought of in nearly forty years. The inscription read, "Do you remember the pony farm?" I was instantly transported back in time. Age, miles, menopause, life, and death had not erased memories so well-etched in my mind that I often still dream of the horses and people who saved my young life. I put the card away. There would be time to think about it later.

I waited until the house was silent and everyone was asleep before I crept downstairs to retrieve the card from so long ago. The Christmas tree lights gave the soft glow I needed to reminisce. I poured a glass of wine and curled up on the old leather couch.

It was the perfect time to invite some cherished old memories back into my life.

I closed my eyes and softly hummed the song that a motley group of preteen girls made up one rainy afternoon. We substituted the lyrics to "We're Poor Little Sheep Who Have Gone Astray" with these words:

> *We're poor little girls who have gone astray / bah, bah, bah / at Still's pony farm where we found our way / bah, bah, bah / Shoveling poop and baling hay / leading horses along the way / hoping for rides that we earn each day / bah, bah, bah.*

What a silly song. We'd come up with it while sitting around on cold metal chairs under a leaky old awning, wrapped in musty horse blankets, surrounded by wet smelly horses, making up songs and playing games to keep our minds off the cold rain that kept us from riding.

Remembering the song, remembering the pony farm, flooded my soul with myriad feelings. That place, those experiences, had literally saved my life. It made me wonder now, *How does one pay adequate tribute to something that powerful?*

The pony farm was about twenty miles northeast of Atlanta. In the center of the farm was a riding ring where parents would bring their children to be led around on horses. The ring was about a quarter of a mile long. Twenty-five cents a ride, four rides for a dollar. Preteen girls, like me, would walk for hours on end leading the "privileged" kids around the ring. We "pony girls" were not privileged. In fact, most of us were considered to be from "the other side of the tracks."

I believe it was more than fate that had prompted my mother to find the small house two blocks from the pony farm. We had already moved six times in the six years since she'd left my father. Mother was constantly shuffling and reshuffling dysfunctional relationships and marriages like a crazy deck of cards. Her male companion preferences tended toward alcoholics and/or emotionally unstable men. The little house was a tenement dump. But to me it was a mansion. At least it was a house and not a run-down apartment. When I discovered the pony farm around the corner, I was ecstatic.

From early childhood I had loved horses. Forget dolls. While other kids were riding bikes, I was riding my homemade stick horse in and out of the alleys of downtown Atlanta. That stick horse and I would ride away from the grimy apartment complexes into perfect worlds—worlds I could create in my imagination.

I remember the first time I walked to the pony farm as clearly as if it were yesterday. I was a shy, skinny, awkward little redhead. What I found at the farm were other shy, skinny, awkward little girls very much like myself—little girls who knew the secrets and fears of homes filled with alcoholism and mental illness. By some miracle we found ourselves at the pony farm, which was, for most of us, the only place we were truly safe; Mrs. Still saw to that.

Mrs. Still—Annie was her first name—seemed very old to us. I don't know when she and Mr. Still began taking in wayward girls. They were gruff and worked us hard, and we adored them. Most of the time they pretended not to know we were spending our nights in the barn; sleeping with horses was far safer than sleeping in our own beds.

My mother rarely knew where I was. I came and went as I pleased. On bad nights, when the violence escalated or my mother disappeared (sometimes being taken away for the next shock treatment), I would simply slip out a window and head to the farm. Curling up in fragrant hay next to a warm horse provided the comfort I needed.

I wasn't the only girl who sought refuge at the farm. Most mornings would find one or two girls curled up in a favorite pony's stall. The smell of coffee always signaled us to come in the house for a good breakfast. In winter, particularly when it was cold, Mrs. Still would drag us out of the barn to sleep in the house. We would tangle ourselves up in old blankets on the living room floor, whispering secrets into the night. We created fantasies of white knights who would sweep us up to live happily ever after—on horse farms, of course.

One year Mr. Still gave me a scrawny-looking bay filly to raise. I named her Shenandoah Fawn. The only requirement was that I pay for her feed. I worked day and night mucking stalls and doing any and every odd job possible to keep up with the bill. I adored that filly and trained her like a dog, teaching her to bow and shake hands. I came to the farm one day to find strangers leading her into a trailer. She had been sold at the request of my mother, and there was nothing the Stills could do, because I was a minor.

In that moment I discovered what it felt like to have a broken heart. No abuse or neglect in my life had hurt as much as seeing that filly being taken away. The compassion and love of the Stills and the other girls helped me to better understand loss and how to walk myself through that kind of pain—a lesson that helped me navigate other painful losses and experiences later in my life.

Memories of the pony farm jolted me back to the present. I wiped tears from my face, jumped off the sofa, and quickly made my way to the mud room. Grabbing my old stable jacket and throwing it over my gown, I pulled on my boots and went outside, quietly closing the door behind me. I walked slowly though the swirling snow to the barn. The horses began to nicker, wondering what in the heck I was doing visiting in the middle of the night. They were, most definitely, hoping for a treat.

As they came in to nuzzle me, I threw my arms around my beloved bay Morgan's neck, burying my head in his thick winter coat. I felt that wonderful familiar warmth that began forty years ago at the pony farm. That farm nurtured a wounded little girl and instilled in her not only a love for horses, but also a determination to overcome adversity and a belief in the ability to fulfill dreams. It helped to give me the foundation with which to build a better life for myself—one that includes a gentle and under-standing husband, loving and healthy children, and terrific grandkids.

That life-saving childhood experience at the pony farm came full circle for me seven years ago when I wrote a check for Callie, a crippled, old quarter horse mare. When I handed her owner the money, saving her from the sale barn, I said to Callie, "No one can ever take you away from me." And they never did. It was as if I had gone back and reclaimed Shenandoah Fawn, and it enabled me to complete a healing process that began at the pony farm.

The purchase of Callie brought me a new and exciting life with horses. My middle-aged friends and I have glorious rides throughout the mountains and canyons of the Southwest. But more important than just enjoying life with horses, when I moved to Colorado I was given the opportunity to work as a psychotherapist, using horses in therapy with disadvantaged youth. I found my own way to help little girls like myself. My life with the pony farm has indeed come full circle.

A simple Christmas card helped me remember—and give thanks for—the horses and people who changed my life: Mr. and Mrs. Still, Major, General, Trigger, Spot, Brownie, Blackie, Molly, Razor, Buckie, and the rest, but especially Shenandoah Fawn and Callie.

Nancy Schaufele

Mercy's Magic

When we got Mercy, a miniature horse with a sweet disposition and a keen intelligence, I figured she'd make a great family pet. And she did. What I hadn't planned on was putting the mare to work. But I did, because we soon learned that she was also great with, and for, people with special needs.

After Mercy became a certified therapy horse, we purchased a small horse trailer to take her to visit people and places. Announcements about Mercy's work in local newspapers and word-of-mouth referrals kept us busy. The experience provided my sons, Andrew and Benjamin, with valuable lessons in volunteering, and they enjoyed the attention surrounding Mercy. Of course, Mercy enjoyed the attention, too. And I enjoyed meeting people and seeing the joy that Mercy's antics and friendliness brought them.

The only problem was my aging car. It first protested by overheating spectacularly on a trip home. My husband fixed the thermostat and said we were ready to go. But I knew the only way to avoid another protest was to stop pushing the old geezer to her limits. That meant cutting back on Mercy's schedule.

Meanwhile, I received a call from the manager of a daycare facility for mentally and physically challenged adults. He had read the newspaper articles about Mercy and thought the center's clients would enjoy meeting her. I booked a date to visit the center, which was in a town I'd rarely visited, almost an hour from our home.

On a warm Wednesday in July, my sons and I hooked the trailer to the car and headed for a friend's farm, where Mercy was boarded. We didn't make it to the end of our road before the temperature gauge "redlined," despite the new thermostat. Although the temperature outside was pushing 90 degrees, I turned the heater on full blast to cool down the engine and drove back home, praying we'd get there before another fountain of antifreeze gushed out from under the hood. We did, but by then I was a cranky, sweaty mess, and my kids were in no better shape.

I called the manager at the adult daycare center to let him know we couldn't make it that day, and we rescheduled for a week later.

My husband added more fluids and then, for good measure, he checked the air pressure in the tires and changed the wiper blades. "Good to go," he said.

The following Wednesday, we attempted the trip again. This time, the engine would not even turn over. I said a few choice words out of earshot of my sons and made another call to the manager of the center.

"Does your husband need the name of a good mechanic?" he asked.

We scheduled a third time, for two weeks later, taking us into August.

Not wanting to blow the visit a third time, I asked the boys what they thought our other options for transporting Mercy might be.

"Do we have to do this?" six-year-old Andrew asked in frustration. "We could be swimming!"

"The people like to see Mercy. She makes them feel better. It's Mercy's magic," his younger brother, Benjamin, said. "Plus, Mom usually gets us a good snack."

For a four-year-old, Benjamin was very wise for his years. Andrew scowled angrily at his brother.

"Do you have an idea on how we might get Mercy to the center, Benjamin?" I asked hopefully.

He looked up thoughtfully, a finger on his chin—a familiar gesture when he wanted something. "Why don't we take Mercy in the car like we used to? The car runs fine when it's not pulling the trailer," Benjamin said. "And we can get ice cream."

"But—" Andy started to object.

"We have no other option, Andy," I said.

Benjamin was right. We were able to get around town in my old Jeep Cherokee when the trailer wasn't attached, and Mercy had ridden in the back before we had the trailer. We'd pull out the backseat, tarp the floor, put hay behind the driver's seat, and open the rear door, and Mercy would jump right in. She would munch hay until we arrived at our destination, and after her visit, she would return to her "seat" for carrots.

"Mercy is going to eat her hay and our ice cream," Andy complained.

"It will work," I said, hopefully.

Everything went as planned until we went to load Mercy and I realized we had a problem: The front passenger seat had one seatbelt; I had two boys.

"We can share," Benjamin offered.

Though I knew it was unsafe, I buckled both boys into the seat; we had no other choice.

Mercy hopped into the back, the car started with no problems, and we were off. The temperature gauge stayed in the normal range, but just to be safe, I drove with the windows down and the heater on full blast.

I had directions on how to get to the facility, but due to a chronic lapse in brain activity when I get into urban areas, I got lost. Tooling around a strange city in 90-degree heat, in an unreliable car, with the heater blazing, two restless boys sharing one seatbelt, a horse in the backseat, and people staring and pointing at Mercy was fraying my nerves. To make matters worse, Mercy kept nudging my shoulder as if to ask, "Are we there yet?"

After 30 minutes of driving around without a clue, I had to ask for directions. I pulled into a strip mall, looking for possibilities. No gas stations were in sight, but there was a hair salon. Ladies in hair salons know everything, so I pulled in front, explained to the boys I was going to ask for directions, and instructed them not to talk to anyone.

"What if a stranger comes?" Andy asked.

"Andy, we have a *horse* in our car. Who is going to talk to us?" Benjamin said.

Andy slumped back and clutched Mercy's lead.

"You behave, Mercy," I instructed the mare as I closed the driver's door.

When I entered the salon, the well-coiffed lady behind the counter lifted a questioning eyebrow at me. I was sweaty and smelled of suntan lotion and horse—obviously not the normal suburban-urban client they were used to.

"I'm lost," I said, looking out the window at my car.

I saw Andrew talking to Mercy, Mercy nodding her head yes, and Benjamin pinning Andrew to the car seat. Then I saw Benjamin talking to Mercy, Mercy again nodding her head yes, and Andrew putting Benjamin in a chokehold.

"How can I help you?" she asked.

"I need the county Department of Social Services. I have an appointment to meet with challenged adults."

Her gaze brightened, probably figuring I was challenged myself. "I see," she said, turning her attention to the front door as it opened.

A well-dressed elderly lady tottered in. She came up to the desk, peering over her shoulder, obviously looking at my car, which was now rhythmically shaking as if illicit behavior was occurring within it. The sun's glare on my windshield hid Andrew, Benjamin, and Mercy, so I could not tell who was beating on whom at the moment.

"Hello, Elaine," the patron said to the receptionist. "I'm early for my appointment. Did you see that strange-looking dog in the car out front?"

Elaine peered back over the desk and adjusted her bifocals to get a better view.

"It's not a dog; it's a horse," I stammered.

They looked at me as if I had stepped off a flying saucer. "Oh, my!" they said in unison and ran out the door to my car.

I was right behind them. When I reached the car, Andrew still had Benjamin in a chokehold, Benjamin was still taunting him, and Mercy was still nodding her head yes. She had been trained to answer questions by nodding her head at one prompt or shaking her head at another.

"All of you, cut it out!" I hissed.

"Andy asked Mercy if I was stupid and made her say yes," Benjamin complained.

"Ben asked Mercy if I was a loser and made her say yes," Andrew whined.

"Did not!"

"Did so!"

"Boys!" I shouted.

Elaine and her client were on the driver's side of the car, poking their fingers at Mercy's nose. Mercy was now shaking her head no in protest. Well-coiffed salon ladies were unfamiliar to her.

"That goes for you, too!" I told Mercy. "Stop it!"

She stopped, blinking her big doe eyes at me innocently.

Finally, the elderly lady gave me directions to the adult daycare center, which was right around the corner. When I pulled into the parking lot, aides and their patients were already waiting, and they cheered as Mercy jumped from the car. I still held her lead, but she was already doing her job of making people happy.

As the people touched the glistening coat and played with the flowing mane of our miniature goodwill ambassador, I forgot about the hassles of getting her there. There were smiles, bright eyes, and happy murmurings all around. The oldest lady in the facility repeatedly hugged Mercy and called out, "I love Mercy! I love Mercy!" Even after her aide took her back inside, she could still be heard calling to Mercy.

Benjamin looked around and smiled. "Mercy's magic," he said. The aides nodded in agreement.

The visit was a success. Even Andrew got involved by having Mercy answer polite questions for the daycare clients. After two hours, we waved goodbye, loaded Mercy into the car, and started down the driveway. What I heard and saw next made my stomach roll.

"Mom!" Andrew screamed, sliding onto the floor in a ball, trying to make it look like Benjamin was the only passenger up front.

"What?" I asked.

He motioned to two police cars and an animal control officer in a truck coming toward us. In this urban area, I doubted they were looking for rabid animals. I pulled over to the side of the road and lifted my state map, hiding behind it. My mind raced. *If someone complained about a horse in the city, what would officials look for? After all, when people say "horse," most folks think of a large animal. That being the case, could we hide Mercy in the car and escape?*

"Benjamin, give Mercy all of the carrots. If we get her head down, she looks like a big dog."

Benjamin nodded and flung the whole bag at Mercy's face. I heard crunching. One problem solved.

The police cars made a left turn, followed by the animal control officer. I put down my map, turned on my left blinker, and went the opposite way, still praying they were looking for a big horse.

A different police car came toward us from another direction.

"Give Mercy the can of grain," I whispered to Benjamin.

"The whole can?"

"Do you want to go to jail?" Andrew asked from the car floor.

Benjamin dumped the can of grain on the floor, and we merged into traffic.

"Sit up," I instructed Andrew.

He got into the seat next to Benjamin and buckled up.

"That was cool," Benjamin said. ". . . Not!"

While I wondered whether all we had gone through to make a group of people happy for two hours was worth it, Mercy nuzzled my shoulder. I reached back for her soft nose. In that moment, I forgot our troubles and just enjoyed having that connection with a tiny horse who enjoyed being with us, even if it was inside a car, and who liked making people, even ones she didn't know, happy.

"Yes," I said with a smile, "Mercy is magic."

Denise J. Pullis

A version of this story was first published under the title "A Great Escape" in (the now defunct) Miniature Horse Voice *magazine, January 2000.*

My $1 Lifesaver

Brego came to our place on April 1, 2005, the day after we had my daughter's very old palomino put down. Brego was his replacement, and at twenty-five years old, he was not a young fellow either. Originally registered in California as Swedish Cat and also named Monkey by previous owners, he needed a statelier name. My daughter called him Brego, which she claimed was a horse of Rohan given to Strider in the movie *The Lord of the Rings*. It seemed fitting, because Strider, who apparently understood and talked to horses in Elfin, said something along the lines of, "This horse tells me he has seen enough of war. Turn him out to pasture."

Our Brego is still pressed into service routinely. He goes for long rides into Oak Hammock Marsh near Winnipeg, Manitoba, takes part in the Interlake Riding Club shows, and belongs to 4-H. He has a girlfriend who boards with us—Katie, a pretty quarter horse—and he becomes distraught when parted from her. His face is the picture of abject tolerance when he is being subjected to having his mane braided; he never complains.

Being as Brego was quite thin when we got him, we fed him a large amount of food twice a day. Because he was in the field with other horses that did not get this special treatment, at mealtimes he had to be let into another corral, so as not to be disturbed. As horses do, the rest of the herd figured this all out and would deliberately crowd around the gate, forcing Brego back, which made him quite agitated. It was our job as the human herd leaders to clear the pests away.

One soggy August morning, I went out with the bowl and put it on the ground inside the safe corral. The jostling crowd was assembled. Brego began pawing the ground impatiently. It is important to note that this horse is actually a fine old gentleman with excellent manners. Who knows why, but that particular day he chose to charge right through those annoying pasture mates and show them who's the boss. I had just opened the gate and was doing my part by shooing the pushy yearlings when Brego launched himself at me to get to his bowl. I was unable to duck completely out of the way due to the slimy ground and to the unexpected quickness of his movement. Brego pushed me with his shoulder, and I fell onto the gate and then onto my knees. Amazed he hadn't stepped on my leg, I got up, brushed myself off, determined I was unhurt, and went on with my day.

Two months later, though, I still had a bruise and a lump on my right breast where I'd been injured when Brego knocked me into the gate. So off I went to the doctor. She and I both felt certain that the bruising and swelling were just a result of the Brego incident. Nevertheless, I was sent for a mammogram. The diagnosis was an unpleasant surprise: I had breast cancer. And it had nothing to do with the bruised area or the lump. As suspected, those came from the accident with Brego and were nothing to worry about. But the tests I'd received for that trauma revealed a very early *ductal carcinoma in situ* deep down in my tissue, near the chest wall. The cells were one step from bursting into full-fledged, lymph-infiltrating cancer. I was lucky!

Lumpectomy and radiation treatments took a total of nine months. Since then, it's been a long road back up to speed, but before long I was back on my own horse, riding around the fields. As always, my daughter comes along on her buddy, Brego. He's very special to me now, too. Every day since I was given that diagnosis and anytime my heart is heavy, I either think of Brego or see him waiting at the gate for his bowl and smile. I remind myself how fortunate I am that he came into our lives and pushed me against that gate. Though he was likely nothing more than an instrument of fate, I still call him my lifesaver.

And to think I only paid a token $1 for him. It's the best dollar I've ever spent. Thanks again, Brego!

Ishbel Moore

This story was first published in Horse Country Magazine, *Jan.-Mar. 2007, Manitoba, Canada.*

Freeing Feetsy

The first time I met Feetsy, she was twenty-five years old, and I thought she looked great for an old gal in her out-to-pasture years. A gorgeous palomino quarter horse and Thoroughbred cross, Fancy Feet had helped raise the children of my good friend, Bonnie.

Before Bonnie's kids were born, she and Feetsy had spent many a morning sailing over jumps in the schooling ring and many an afternoon heading out on the trails for more of the same. Several years had passed since they had taken those rides through the woods. Over the years, even their visits grew fewer and farther apart, especially after Bonnie became a single mom to a trio of young kids. Still, anyone could see that the bond the two had forged when they were young was still powerful and true.

When Bonnie's mom passed away, part of the process of clearing her estate involved finding a new home for Feetsy, who had been spending her days peacefully in a small pasture behind her house. Though my veterinary practice is exclusively small animal, I have horses of my own and had a few contacts in the horse business. So I was lucky to secure a place for Feetsy with a small boarding facility that already had a number of "retired" mares and geldings. I knew the owners fairly well and was confident Feetsy would get the type of special attention she needed at that point in her life.

Even though our work schedules and other obligations left little time for socializing, Bonnie and I still managed to get together regularly to raid the bookshelves at Walden's before taking in a movie and popcorn. During one such girl's night out, Bonnie asked if I would go out to the boarding barn with her and take a look at Feetsy.

"I think it might be time to put her down," she said. "Could you come out after work and look at her, just to tell me what you think?"

My heart sank as I thought of what losing Feetsy would mean to Bonnie and her children. "What's going on?" I asked. "Is she lame? Has she been sick, colicky, not eating . . . ?"

Bonnie shook her head. "She's getting around okay. She's lost some weight; she can't really chew grass or hay, so they have to make her a gruel out of senior feed and beet pulp three times a day. She's been dewormed and everything. I don't know. She's just not right."

"You know I'm not a horse vet, but I'd be glad to take a look," I said. "We could draw some blood and give Dr. Lari a call if anything shows up."

I met Bonnie at the barn a few evenings later. We headed up the short trail through the woods to the small pasture Feetsy shared with another cross-bred mare and a few pushy ponies. At one end of the pasture was a single row of stalls set up like a run-in shed, with doors on both sides that normally stayed open. Feetsy was in her stall, slurping her dinner, and the stall doors were closed to keep out the ponies.

I took a quick look around. There were a couple of troughs holding clean water, a few nontoxic weeds, and a decent stand of spring grass pushing it's way up through the rocky soil of the pasture. The other horses had already eaten and were clearly hanging around to see who the new people were and to lap up any of Feetsy's leftovers. When Feetsy finished eating, we opened the stall doors, and she trudged out of one while the pushy ponies raced in the other. After watching the old girl walk around a bit, my impression wasn't so much of a horse that was lame or weak, but rather one that was depressed. She showed little interest in her surroundings, other than to swat her long tail at the pesky flies that continually tried to land on her sweat-soaked coat.

"Let's draw some blood, see if there's something obvious going on metabolically, then we'll go from there," I suggested.

The lab results were remarkably unremarkable. That's vet speak for "not helpful at all" when you're hoping something will point toward a diagnosis.

A few days later, Bonnie called to tell me that the folks who had been taking care of Feetsy the past four years were getting ready to retire and sell the property. The suggestion was made that Bonnie should either find another place for Feetsy or consider putting her down. For Bonnie, there really was no choice. Moving Feetsy to a larger facility would create a financial burden. But she wasn't ready to say goodbye to this mare who had been such an important part of her life for nearly thirty years.

So I contacted Debbie and Blanchard, the owners of the breeding/training facility where I regularly schooled my mare and where she occasionally stayed during show season. We discussed Feetsy's feeding regimen; it would mean taking a little extra time and care, but it was doable. They were willing to take Feetsy on my recommendation, give us a fair assessment of her condition, and, if feasible, keep her for as long as she seemed comfortable and happy—whether that meant days or months or longer, we had no way of knowing.

Feetsy had her Coggins, and off she went to her new home. Well, it wasn't quite that easy. There was a moment of panic as we started to load her onto my trailer. Feetsy hesitated, and I thought, *This could be a very long night.* I gave her a little tap on the rump. I looked at Bonnie. Bonnie looked at Feetsy. Feetsy gave Bonnie a slightly startled look out of her big, brown eyes, then she stepped right up into the trailer, and the butt bar flew into its slot behind her. There are some things a well-trained horse just never forgets.

Fancy Feet's first few days at her new home were spent in a well-ventilated stall near Pattrinka, my Arabian mare, and Charity, an aged Morgan mare. After the first day or two, Feetsy was eating better, and the decision was made to let her stay in the stall during the heat of the day and then move her out to share pasture space with a handful of other mares in the evenings, so long as they seemed to get along. If the days were tolerable, she could stay out during the day as well. Bonnie made regular visits during that first week, and I was hopeful all would work out well for my friends.

For people who don't know or care for horses, it's hard for those of us who do to describe the feeling you get from watching horses "at play" in an open field. Like so many others who believe that the outside of a horse is good for the inside of a person, I've spent countless hours sitting on fences watching foals play hide-and-seek with their moms or tag with their pasture buddies. Or watching yearlings racing each other to gates to see who can greet the newcomers first and then chasing the newcomers around the pasture in between staging mock battles (or real ones!) to see who's gonna be top dog. Or watching that young stallion at the breeding barn who finally gets his turn to enjoy a few hours of turnout and explodes in a burst of exuberant energy as he races and bucks and snorts and prances his way around the paddock, making sure everyone sees how handsome and what a great mover he is.

So maybe those of you who appreciate the beauty of such moments will understand why I had tears in my eyes the next time I saw Feetsy.

It was a Saturday morning. I had finished my rounds at the clinic and was looking forward to a good schooling session with my mare and to seeing how Feetsy was settling in at her new home. The tree-lined drive at the entrance to the training/breeding complex is bordered on both sides by pasture, and as I pulled into the drive and looked to the right where I knew my mare would be, I couldn't believe my eyes. Feetsy and Trinka were in the pasture with two yearling fillies. As I drove by, Feetsy started racing around the other horses, bucking and kicking up her heels like a two-year-old, as if to say, "Look at me! I feel good!" It was incredible. I had to look twice to make sure it was the same horse who had stood in her stall so forlorn just the week before.

In the days and weeks that followed, Feetsy continued to improve. She put on weight, and her coat, which had stayed heavy and unkempt through the previous summer, began to shed and look brighter and healthier. She acted like a much younger horse, and it was her attitude that prompted Blanchard to suggest to Bonnie that she might want to consider riding Feetsy again.

"Really?" Bonnie asked. "Do you think it would be alright? I wouldn't want to hurt her."

"Sure, I don't see why not," Blanchard replied. "She's fairly well-muscled, remarkably sound, and obviously has loads of energy. As long as you take it slow, give her time to build up her back, and make sure she's comfortable, it would be fine."

Bonnie was ecstatic. Although that first ride around the indoor arena lasted only about five minutes and consisted of the two of them just walking around and getting a feel for each other again, I swear that horse's grin was as wide as Bonnie's. Following Blanchard's advice, Bonnie kept things slow and easy until it was obvious that Feetsy was capable of handling a little more work. Eventually, Trinka and I invited the two of them to join us out on the trails.

In late November, Bonnie and I made plans for another trail ride on Friday, the day after Thanksgiving. We'd ridden together the previous Saturday, and Feetsy was actually pushing my mare along, as if she had places to go and things to do and we weren't getting there fast enough to suit her. It had been awesome watching Bonnie and Feetsy having so much fun together. So when the phone rang as I was getting ready that Friday morning, I hoped nothing had happened to keep us from another great ride. But when I heard Bonnie's tight voice on the other end of the line, I knew something was terribly wrong.

"Feetsy went down this morning. Dr. Lari's not sure what's wrong yet, but Feetsy's in a lot of pain and the meds don't seem to be helping. I'm afraid we're going to have to put her down."

No words would comfort her. I rushed to finish my barn chores and headed to the training center, but by the time I arrived, Feetsy was gone and Bonnie had left to grieve at home.

I knew Bonnie was not only mourning the loss of her friend, she was also berating herself for "pushing" her mare and possibly hastening her end. So, as a vet and as her friend, I reassured her that she hadn't done anything to harm Feetsy. In fact, she had helped her by enabling her to enjoy the last six months of her life. Finally, Bonnie began to glimpse what everyone around her could so clearly see: that she'd given Fancy Feet a new life, the chance to be a horse again, to frolic with her new equine friends and to be Bonnie's partner in the saddle again.

On a wall at my clinic hangs a framed photo of two mature dogs cavorting on a beach. Below the picture is a quote from George Bernard Shaw that reads, "We don't stop playing because we grow old; we grow old because we stop playing." Feetsy taught all of us the truth in that . . . because Bonnie made sure that her mare's last days were filled with fun and friendship.

Libby McKay, DVM

The Backyard Race

I had ridden before, but never like this.

I had always felt at home on a horse. Growing up, I went to riding stables whenever I got the chance, and those chances didn't come nearly often enough for my liking. Like millions of freckled-faced little girls, I wanted a horse so badly it drove me up a tree . . . literally. I was an avid climber, and one day when I was about seven, I took to the highest branch of an old elm in the backyard and told my parents I wasn't coming down until they bought me a horse. It didn't work. The sun went down, determination gave way to hunger, and I gave up my strike, but not my dream. It lived on into my twenties, though by then my riding opportunities were few and far between.

So when a friend called one warm, cloudless day to invite me to go horseback riding at his farm, it was an offer I couldn't refuse. Though I was more than a little rusty, I jumped at the chance to get back in the saddle again. Within minutes of hanging up the phone, I was at the barn and tacking up a horse named Ginger, while my friend threw a saddle on Blaze. Both were quarter horses with enough Arabian in them to keep things interesting.

My friend led the way out of the corral, away from the barn, and across a grassy field. My body absorbed the movement of the horse's feet, and the sun threw its blessing down on my face and shoulders. We passed an old farm house, a corn field, and a herd of cattle. This was the life. I could think here. I could relax. I could breathe.

My normal life didn't include such luxuries. I was burning the candle at both ends, working an accounting job during the week and as a rookie producer of a television news station on the weekends. I was a newlywed, and in moments of honesty, I could admit to myself that things weren't going as perfectly as I had envisioned. This day, this ride, was the release I needed.

Several minutes into the ride I could feel something change in Ginger's behavior. The horses had been walking with a good bit of distance between them, but now Ginger began to close the gap. Her breathing became audible as she let out each breath with deliberate force.

"We're getting ready to go up this hill," my friend explained. "A little ways up, we'll come to a long, flat area. Do you want to race from there to the top?"

The question was asked with a slight grin. He knew I hadn't raced a horse anywhere, much less uphill, before, and he knew that I was a bit of a chicken when it came to speed. Roller coasters, motorcycles, and bungee jumping weren't exactly on my list of things to do, and I wasn't one to cave in to peer pressure. But this was different. This was riding, and I wasn't about to show any fear.

"Sure!" I tried to sound enthusiastic, but my voice squeaked out about an octave above normal.

My friend just nodded, smiled again, and turned back around. We headed up the hill, each step coming a little more quickly. Ginger's ears were now turned completely forward, and she and Blaze were side by side as we came up to the flat ground.

"Ready?"

I willed my lips to smile. "Ready."

I don't even know if I squeezed my legs. I probably just thought about it. That's all Ginger needed. We went from walk to gallop in a heartbeat. My hair flew out behind me like a banner. Her feet thundered on the ground, and I could feel her muscles pushing her on, straining to keep pace with the younger Blaze. I held the reins in one hand and as much mane as

I could weave through my fingers with the other. Wind whistled in my ears as we covered ground by barely touching it, leaping off one stride to the next. At some point I lost my right stirrup and struggled to keep my balance for a few seconds, until, by some miracle, my boot made its way back in. Then, just as quickly as it began, it was over. Ginger was a horse-length behind as the path narrowed, and we were forced to trot, then walk, then halt.

I loved it! I loved every part of it. The speed, the noise, even the fear, all jumbled up to create a feeling of being alive, of being free. There was nothing like it. This backyard race was a drug, and I was an immediate addict.

From then on, I rode as often as possible. I got up early and rode before work. I sped home and rode before it got dark. I spent time just sitting in the middle of the pasture, watching Ginger graze and thinking about the next time. It became my therapy, my time to heal, my moments of complete freedom.

A few months later, I called a friend of mine. She'd told me she liked horses and had ridden as a child but hadn't been in the saddle in years. It didn't take long for me to convince her to meet me at the barn.

The morning light shone through the trees as we took the now-familiar walk around the old farmhouse and the corn field. The cattle barely turned from their hay as we strolled by their pasture. A few minutes later, we came upon the hill that led up to that flat piece of land, now marked with hundreds of hoof prints and just as many memories.

I turned in the saddle with a grin on my face and mischief in my eyes.

"Wanna race?"

Robyn Keeney

Attached

It was midnight, and I was in the street with my mom banging dustbin lids. Our neighbors were there, too, with whistles, rattles, and tin cans. Adding a bass section were all the ships in the nearby docks blowing their foghorns. It sounded like everyone in London was bashing, blowing, or blasting a welcome to the new decade—the sixties. With such fanfare, I felt sure that New Year's Day would bring with it a shiny new world, but the only difference was that the next morning the milkman tripped over our dustbin lid, startling his horse and making all the bottles in the milk cart jingle. The milkman shouted at his horse, and I was awake early.

Raymond, our milkman, had a horse that fascinated me. She didn't need Raymond holding the reigns or leading her; she knew all the houses that got milk and stopped outside them. All Raymond had to do was get the bottles off the back of the cart, put them on the doorsteps, and walk to the next house. Raymond wasn't satisfied with his talented horse, however, and was always muttering under his breath, complaining about something or other. The horse would whinny and shake her head, as though she understood but disagreed.

My mom told me that Raymond and his horse started squabbling toward the end of the Second World War. The cause of the quarrel was the house at number 132. A customer, Mrs. Gotobed, had lived there until a flying bomb blew it up. "Doodlebugs," everyone called them. They traveled faster than the speed of sound. If you heard one coming, you were probably safe, because it would be going someplace else. Mrs. Gotobed never heard the doodlebug coming, and it blew her and number 132 sky-high. Raymond's horse learned quickly which houses did not get milk, but she never came to terms with houses exploding overnight, so every time she reached number 132, she stopped. It drove Raymond crazy.

"Stupid 'orse! 'ow many times do I 'ave to say it, 'Don't stop at number 132!' Can't you see, there's no blooming house there? It's grass, a bombsite, an empty space. I'm putting in for one of those new fangled 'lectric carts and sending you to the glue factory."

Most people in East London in those days lived in terraced houses, side-by-side buildings that shared the same sidewalls. They had tiny front gardens, only big enough to keep bikes in.

I said to my mom, "Maybe it's because the horse has been surrounded by bricks and concrete all her life, and when she suddenly gets a whiff of Mrs. Gotobed's grass and flowers that have spread all over the bombsite, some long-faded memory drifts across her mind and she stops for a little dream of wide-open prairies."

But Mom said, "You watch too many cowboy films. That horse stops at one-thirty-two each morning because all through the war Mrs. Gotobed gave it a cookie every day, despite no one else on the street being able to get cookies because of the war."

When I started a newspaper delivery round, some days I finished as Raymond was on his way back to his depot, and he would give me a lift. I was thirteen years old but felt grown up sitting up there in the cab next to Raymond.

"How does your horse remember which houses to stop at, Raymond? That's pretty clever."

"Clever? I've never met such a stupid 'orse. No, she ain't clever, lad. In fact, it'd be a lot easier with a 'lectric cart; I wouldn't 'ave to get up in the middle of the night and feed the bag of bones before we came out or calm the stupid thing down every time there's a rumble of thunder in the air. And I wouldn't have to tell her every single day that number one-thirty-two no longer wants a half pint of milk."

At that time, I had gained the little knowledge I did have of horses from comics, films, and television. I thought that the heroic adventures of *Champion the Wonder Horse* were everyday things for a horse and that if Raymond was ever tied to the nearby railway line by a gang of outlawed milkmen, Raymond would have only to whistle and his horse would be there, rearing up on her hind legs, scattering the baddies to all parts of London. Then she'd bite through the ropes just in time for Raymond to roll free as the 3.10 to Liverpool Street came thundering by. I knew that I should have stood up for the horse, considering that she was the smartest animal I knew, but I was only thirteen and was overwhelmed by being in Raymond's milk cart and being part of the grownup world.

"What's your horse's name?" I asked.

"Name? She ain't got a name, lad. She's just 'orse. You see, it wouldn't do to give an 'orse a name, lad; you'd end up getting attached to it. Then where'd you be?"

I nodded, but I couldn't imagine what was wrong with being attached to a horse. I didn't want to spoil the chumminess of the moment by disagreeing, though, so I went along with Raymond again.

Later, when I started work proper, I'd wait for Raymond and his horse to trip by each morning and then I'd know it was time for work. One morning I awoke with a start. I thought I was still dreaming, because I could hear the sound of galloping hooves. I jumped out of bed and looked out the window just in time to see Raymond's horse galloping down the road. Past 132, past our house, the milk cart swaying from side to side, bottles flying off the back, leaving a wake of white splodges all down the road. Then, as she had for the previous twenty years, she turned sharp right onto Coronation Road and out of sight. There was a moment of silence followed by a crash, like a bottle factory falling from the sky. Then Raymond came running down the road, red-faced, his moneybag streaming out from his shoulder.

When I got there, the milk cart was over on its side by Marshall's corner store and the horse was still in the shafts on her side. Raymond was kneeling amongst the broken glass in a pool of spilt milk, holding the horse in his arms, as best he could hold a half-ton horse in his arms. The horse's eyes were wild, nostrils flaring, and she was making a sort of crying noise from deep inside. Raymond had tears in his eyes as he said, "Stupid blooming 'orse!"

Mr. Marshall put his hand on Raymond's shoulder. "Leave her now, Raymond. I've called for the vet; he'll sort things out. There's nothing you can do."

But Raymond just repeated, "Stupid blooming 'orse."

Mr. Marshall left Raymond with his horse.

"Terrible thing, son," he said to me. "He's been with that horse since before you were born, through all the air raids and bombing. They never missed a day."

"Do you think there was a storm in the air?" I asked. "Raymond said that thunder sometimes scared her."

"No, son, after all this time, I reckon she just couldn't take it any more."

A year later, I met Raymond walking down our street, looking older and lost without his hat, moneybag, and horse.

"You never did put in for an electric cart, Raymond?" I asked.

"No, lad, I took one out for a trial, but. . . . " He stopped and paused, staring at the new smart house that had been built at number 132 as he shook his head and muttered "stupid blooming 'orse" under his breath.

Finally, he went on. "You see, lad, the thing is, I couldn't see myself ever becoming attached to a 'lectric cart."

When we reached my gate, I said goodbye and watched him continue down the road. He stopped by Marshall's corner store, turned, and called back, "Juliet!"

"What?" I said.

"Juliet! The 'orse. That was 'er name."

Then he walked down Coronation Road, and I never saw him again.

Now, every time I hear bottles rattle in a crate or catch the sound of hooves on the road early in the morning, the memory comes flickering back down the years: the squabble breaking out at number 132, two pints of milk clinking on our step, and a horse taking off down Coronation Road. I suppose, over the years, I've become attached to Raymond and his horse.

Graham E. Rogers

A Birthday Story

Trevor blew out the eight candles on his birthday cake with one big breath. Grinning from ear to ear, he watched the smoke rise into the light hanging above the kitchen table while his parents and party guests applauded. After the cake and presents, the kids wandered off to the den to play with Trevor's new cache of toys. When things settled a bit, Trevor's mom took his dad by the hand, and they walked out to the barn to feed the horses. After completing their evening chores, the couple stood at Posi's stall for a few moments, enjoying the peaceful time and listening to the calming rhythm of the horses chewing hay. This had become their favorite time of day, because they could be alone together and feed horse cookies to their miracle mare, Posi.

For many years, Trevor's parents, Bonnie and Keith, had been DINKs: Double Income No Kids—

professionals with a small horse farm near Sodus Bay on Lake Ontario. They had discussed starting a family several times over the years, but it seemed that restoring their old farm and traveling with their horses filled their lives instead. Then Posi came along.

One spring day nine years earlier, Doc Murray told the couple that Tiva was in foal. Tiva was Bonnie's first horse, a Polish Arabian mare with a breeder's dream pedigree. Bonnie had always wanted a foal from her, but after numerous unsuccessful attempts and considering Tiva's advancing age, they were ready to call it quits. So the old vet's news was cause for celebration and some caution.

Bonnie and Keith attended to Tiva with the utmost care throughout her pregnancy. They gave her fresh water daily and the best hay and feed they could find. She was turned out every morning for exercise and received regular medical checkups. But, with only a few weeks remaining, Tiva started having chronic infections.

Doc Murray said it was due to her female confirmation. "There is a risk she'll reject the fetus," he said matter-of-factly one Saturday.

Bonnie and Keith looked at each other in disbelief. They had waited years for this foal.

"Now don't go frettin' over this," the old vet said reassuringly. "The closer she gets to her due date, the better your chances for a live foal. We'll put her on antibiotics; she'll be fine."

Bonnie and Keith wanted to hope for the best, but after so many disappointments, deep down inside they were ready for the worst.

The doc handed Keith a scribbled prescription for antibiotics. "She shouldn't be lying down until she's ready to deliver. I suggest you keep her tied in her stall for the last few weeks." As the doc took leave, he told them to call him when the mare went into labor.

They followed the vet's orders to a tee. Tiva did not like being tied in a stall, but she tolerated it.

"She's not a happy camper and she's waxing," Keith reported when he came back from the barn one rainy night.

Bonnie got out of bed, grabbed her flashlight, and made her way to the barn.

What they found was not good. Somehow, in the short time it had taken Keith to come in from the barn, the incredibly pregnant mare had found a way to lie down when she was tied. Tiva was cast in her stall. Bonnie unsnapped her tie and tried in vain to pull the helpless mare around so she could stand.

"Call the vet!" she yelled. "Call the vet!"

The time had arrived for Tiva to give birth. Bonnie and Keith both watched nervously as the vet palpated the mare. There was a problem. The foal had no movement. Doc Murray determined that the foal had died in the womb. He conjectured that as the mare had flailed the umbilical cord had wrapped around the foal's neck and cut off blood circulation. Keith and Bonnie were devastated.

Bonnie ran to the house, crying. Keith stayed with Tiva as a drug was administered that would force the mare to deliver. Then the vet left.

Keith sat alone on a bale of straw, elbows on his knees and his head in his hands, waiting for the drug to take effect. He struggled to accept the tragic turn of events. He felt angry, sad, guilty, and confused all at the same time. He wanted to be with Bonnie, but he knew now was not the time. So there he sat, waiting, listening to the raindrops hit the metal roof of the barn.

After what seemed like an eternity, the mare started to stir and make grunting noises. Knowing it was time, Keith went into the stall to assist in the unpleasant task of delivering the dead foal. The feet emerged, then the head, then part of the tiny horse. Keith paused, reached deep for inner strength, then grabbed the front legs and pulled out the foal. Angrily, he tossed the lifeless body in the corner of the stall as the mare looked on. Numb from the events, he wiped his hands on his jeans and turned to head toward the house.

But as he was reaching for the stall door, he heard a funny noise and then rustlings from the corner. He turned and looked in disbelief as a baby horse scrambled in the straw and stood up. Tiva got up, too, and hummered to her newborn. He watched in amazement as nature took over and the foal wobbled across the stall and began suckling its mother.

It was alive! Stunned by what he just witnessed, all he could say was, "Holy cow!" He ran to the house, fumbled to open the screen door, tripped on the threshold, and called out, "It's alive! Bonnie, it's alive!"

He ran back out to the barn and into the stall to look under the tail. It was a filly! Winded, he ran back to the house to tell Bonnie. They met halfway and hugged each other in the warm evening rain.

"It's alive, and it's a filly!" Keith said, panting.

Bonnie grabbed his shoulders and looked Keith in the eye. "Are you sure?"

"I'm positive!" he said as his eyes welled with tears.

They decided to call the filly Positiew, which in Polish means "positive." Her barn name became Posi.

As fate would have it, Bonnie gave birth to her only child, Trevor, nine months later to the day.

Edward Varno

When Shawna Met Sonny

I looked up from washing breakfast dishes and couldn't help but smile at what I saw out my kitchen window. The sunny June day with its brilliant blue sky was enough to lift anyone's spirits. But what prompted my joy at that moment was the sight of a big bay horse grazing in the pasture with a young girl stretched out on his back, reading a book, her elbows propped on his rum. Her ponytail, almost as dark as the horse's mane, hung over one shoulder, and she looked so peaceful and relaxed that it made me sigh out loud.

The girl was my daughter, Shawna—lovely, precious, and as difficult as a fourteen-year-old can be. Overnight she'd changed from a happy, giggling bundle of gangly legs and ponytails into a discontented, rebellious stranger, whom, it seemed, nothing and no one could please . . . that is, until Sonny entered her life.

Sonny was the bay gelding. His story still brings me to tears. Sonny was raised by a good friend and riding partner of my husband's, Bob. A quarter horse-Thoroughbred cross, Sonny showed the best traits of both. Standing 16.5 hands, he was heavily muscled and broad-chested with beautiful brown eyes and a gentle, willing personality.

Bob raised and sold horses for a living. Once his colts were well broken, he'd begin looking for good homes for them. Four years earlier, Sonny had been one of those colts. He went to a young couple as a pleasure horse. Unfortunately, his owners split up, and selling the horse was part of the divorce settlement. Someone told the couple that meat canners were paying top dollar for horses and that they paid by the pound. A big horse like Sonny would bring a good price. The couple obviously had not formed an attachment to the horse, because they made arrangements to have him picked up and sent to the canner. The story could have ended there.

But fate stepped in when Bob found himself in the area and decided to stop in and visit the young couple. He was horrified when he heard what was going on and immediately offered to match the canner's price. He loaded Sonny in his trailer and got him out of there as quickly as possible.

Bob stopped by our house on his way home and over a cup of coffee related the story. He said that Sonny had been neglected for some time and that it would take a while to get him back in shape before he could be resold, but he hoped to find a loving home for him as soon as possible. He remarked how, despite being neglected, the horse had maintained his sweet spirit and seemed to trust anyone who gave him the slightest bit of attention. Just as Bob finished the sad tale, I saw Shawna slip outside.

Bob finished his coffee, and my husband and I walked him out to his pickup. There we found our daughter draped over the back of the bay, still in the trailer, crying her heart out, her face buried in his tangled mane. Sonny was nuzzling her and nickering softly.

It didn't take a rocket scientist to see what many would call a match made in heaven. Neither girl nor animal understood what they were going through, but they did seem to recognize that they had something in common. Bob knew we were not in the market for another horse and that, even if we were, we couldn't afford this one. But he walked right up to the trailer and asked Shawna if she would be willing to nurse Sonny back to good health. Bob told her the horse would need daily grooming and exercise and a good and regular diet and that he had his hands full with his stock at home. Not surprisingly, she jumped at the opportunity.

The horse was promptly unloaded, and the lead rope handed over to Shawna, whose face glowed with an excitement I hadn't seen in some time. With the teen sneer gone, I glimpsed the sweetness I had been missing in my little girl.

Over the next few months, the girl and the horse became inseparable. Sonny flourished under Shawna's care. His coat began to shine. He gained weight. His mane and tail were brushed until they hung wavy and thick. More often than not, he sported a line of braids tied at the end with colored ribbon, but he didn't seem to mind this bit of feminine fancy. Bob stopped by now and then to check on Sonny and usually had a long conversation with Shawna, coaching her and praising her for the hard work and the obviously positive results.

I wondered if Bob saw the change in the girl, too. I surely did. The light in her eyes, the lift of her chin, her laughter—these things I had so missed were slowly returning. Several times, I slipped out to the barn unnoticed to give the horse praise and encouragement for the way he was restoring Shawna's spirit, helping her to once again feel confident and content.

My husband and I cautioned Shawna not to become too attached. But privately we rejoiced in the relationship we saw developing. Shawna and Sonny spent hours together. If she wasn't riding him, she was grooming him or petting him or sitting on the fence talking to him. All of that fourteen-year-old angst that we couldn't drag from her she poured out in torrents to that big bay. And Sonny listened, patiently and nonjudgmentally.

Bob came by less and less often. When questioned about Sonny's prospects, he just said he hadn't found anyone interested in buying the horse yet. He never did.

It's been three years since Bob stopped by for a cup of coffee and left his rescued horse behind for a short respite under the tender loving care of a distressed teen. In the process, that big, shiny, four-legged bay provided my little girl with a steady bridge across the most turbulent of the teen years. And I thank God for him every day.

Cheryl Dale

Bummer and Gypsy

aught up in the heady scents of sweet grass, leather, and fly spray, I flinched when the harsh crack of a whip cut through the lazy spring morning. A group of lathered racehorses flew around a small oval track. My friend Sara and I stopped to check our directions.

"Scott Stables. This is the place," Sara said, as she widened her blue eyes and shook her head at the dismal scene. The side-to-side movement sent waves of honey spilling across her shoulders.

"Are you sure?" I wrinkled my nose in reaction to the offensive odors drifting from the barn and peered through a stall window. "It looks like a tornado hit in there."

Sara shrugged and turned to enter. "It's racing season; maybe they haven't had time to clean stalls or pick up the equipment yet."

I cocked one eyebrow at her as I stepped around a pitchfork leaning against a wheelbarrow.

According to Sara's farrier, the horses sectioned off on this side of the barn were waiting to be hauled away to the glue factory. A black Thoroughbred kicked at the stall and showed teeth.

"Are you sure starting off like this is a good idea?" I asked.

"Cheri, they're the same as the horses you ride at my house." Sara reached out to pat the black horse's velvety muzzle. Snap! She pulled her hand back from his nipping choppers. "They, ah, just need a little more work."

I sighed. "A little more work?"

"Quit whining. You're ten times the rider I am; it must be that Cherokee blood." She narrowed angelic blue eyes, giving me a disgusted look.

"It's been a while since I did this, like twenty years. My idea was to start off nice and easy, not to end up in a body cast."

"Listen to you—"

"Oh, no! Look at that poor mare." I pointed to a huge bay Thoroughbred cross-tied at the end of the barn. The open doors behind the mare let in fresh air and sunshine, a welcome addition to the dreary setting. The bright light intensified her horrible condition.

I approached the bay slowly. Tears filled my eyes as I ran a hand over her protruding hipbones. Raw, infected wounds marked her forehead and cheekbone. I rested my head against her sun-warmed fur for a moment, trying to control my growing anger. While I examined the injured mare, a pulse began to throb in my temples.

The horse nickered.

"Hi, beauty," I said. Gently moving my hands around her soft mouth, I coaxed her to open. "Wow, she's still so young, around seven years old."

"I'd have guessed closer to twenty." Sara said. "The owner, Mr. Scott, sends them out to slaughter if they don't cut it on the track. He's been in the hospital fighting some kind of cancer. I don't think he's responsible for abusing these animals."

"How did you find out about the horses?"

"Glenna, my farrier, used to shoe Scott's horses, but stopped after she witnessed how the new guy treated them. I don't know what his name is, but he shows up drunk all the time. The booze and his temper make a bad combination for the horses. From what Glenna says, he doesn't do much at the track with them. I'm not sure whether he's allowed in."

"Does Mr. Scott know what's going on?"

"I don't know. Glenna only mentioned it when I asked her to watch for some decent horses for you."

"I'm not sure I like Scott any more than the guy that is hurting these horses. Can he destroy perfectly beautiful animals just because they don't win races? Is that legal?"

"Like it or not, it's a business, Cheri, and these places pay for the horsemeat. It is legal, and unfortunately, it is usually what happens. I don't like it either, but I thought you might find something special here. You can pick up a mare with great bloodlines for very little money. I knew it would fit your budget."

I shuddered and gazed into the mare's wide-spaced intelligent eyes, imploring me for help. She was a dark bay with a small white star on her pretty face and stood at an impressive height of 17 hands. She stood swishing her straggly black tail, a few loose strands scattered from the uneven clumps that remained. She stretched out a graceful neck and rested her heavy head on my shoulder, snorting softly in my ear.

I stroked her carefully, avoiding the places that were injured. My fingers stumbled when I found printed letters stamped on her faded green halter.

"Her name is Gypsy."

Sara laughed. "Gypsy knows a sucker when she sees one."

I reached toward my pocket. "Very funny, Sara."

"Go ahead," she smirked. "Feed her those carrots you've got in there before—"

Heated whinnies interrupted our conversation. The pitch rose to wild screams. The sounds ricocheted through the barn from outside. A man's cry for help followed. Gypsy's eyes rolled back in her head in response to his voice.

Sara and I raced outside, but quickly skidded to a stop as we came around the barn. My stomach recoiled from the sight of a small standardbred gelding trapped in a river of electrified fencing. I scanned the gelding's paddock area, trying to figure out what had happened. The two-tiered fencing was connected to the backside of the barn in a U-shaped design; some of the posts holding the wires had fallen to the ground, creating a pool of live wire.

The source of the problem stepped forward. A short, stocky man blocked the gelding's only escape. He gripped the plastic gate handles, jerking the metal wire onto the gelding's back.

The plastic handles acted as a barrier for the man holding them, but the horse shrieked from the contact with the current on the other. The wires on the ground surrounded them, and the horse had no place to run.

While Sara and I watched in horror, electricity snapped through the quivering chestnut's body.

"Stop that!" I screamed.

The terrified horse lurched up, balancing on his hind legs, and knocked off one of the wires, trapping the man who used it. A thick, white, foam coated the lower half of the gelding's body. He reared back, nearly flipping over in an attempt to rid himself of the remaining wire.

I spied a lead line on the ground and glanced up. The gelding still wore his halter. A jagged white stripe ran down his face, resembling a lightning bolt.

"Sara, grab a bucket and put some grain in it!" I yelled over the commotion.

Sara stood frozen.

"Sara," I tried again. "Look at me."

She shook her head and then met my eyes.

"Find a bucket. They were hanging by the stall doors. Put a handful of grain in it. Hurry!"

Picking up the lead line, I hid it behind me and clucked to the horse to get his attention away from the injured man, now pinned against the barn. I pulled out a handful of carrots and held them out, while using my other hand to tuck the lead line in the back pocket of my jeans.

"What a pretty boy," I crooned, inching closer.

He showed teeth, his eyes wild, and pinned his ears. The gelding's sweat-soaked copper sides heaved.

His ragged breathing quickened as I approached. The chestnut snorted. Crimson-stained nostrils flared while he tried to find a way around the fence that snapped on the ground beside him.

Current hummed through the wire, which still held contact with the gelding's hindquarters. He jumped and backed closer to the screaming man, who had blood dripping from his hand. The chestnut's movement nearly dislodged the remaining wire, but it snagged in his tail.

Whispering soft reassurances to the standardbred, I kept moving and tried to reach the end of the yellow plastic handle that was lying on the ground. The red-handled wire resting on top of his tail was intertwined with the second wire on the ground. I hoped to rid him of both, but I needed to distract him for a second.

I threw the carrots on the ground. When the gelding turned his head, I dove for the handle. Grabbing it, I lifted it up and over his tail. The gelding stepped free, and I tossed the offending wires out of harm's way.

"Please, lady," the short balding man called. "Get me outta here! I'm gonna shoot that sum bitch right tween the eyes."

"The horse isn't the one who needs to be shot," I sputtered.

"Lemme out!" he bellowed.

The gelding reared up, striking out with his front legs. My heart hardened as I studied the belligerent man trapped behind the angry horse. For a moment I considered leaving and allowing the irate gelding to finish the man off.

The chestnut lifted his robust head and studied me with tired, wounded eyes. He stopped thrashing and locked his large brown eyes on mine. I stepped toward him slowly, speaking in low, even tones. His breathing was rapid, but he didn't flinch when I ran my hands over his sweaty neck. Tugging the lead line from my pocket, I clipped it on the ring of his halter. Somehow, I knew he wouldn't hurt me.

I stroked him. "Hi, baby, wanna come home with me?"

He snorted in agreement.

I clucked once, starting off on my right foot, praying the gelding would follow.

He took a few steps and stopped. A stubborn look came over his face.

"What's his name?" I called out to the man hugging the barn wall.

"Bum," he hollered back. "Bummer."

I rolled my eyes and clucked again. "Come on, Bummer. No wonder you're touchy. Let's get out of here."

Sara dropped the grain bucket and ran to help the man into the barn. While they were gone, I walked Bummer in small circles, trying to cool him down.

A little later, Sara followed the limping man back outside; he stayed clear of the area where Bummer and I walked. A blue leg wrap encased his hand, its ends tied around his shoulder in a make-shift sling. Wincing, he stopped to rub his leg and watched me working with Bummer.

"Hey, can you hold him there until the meat wagon gets here?" he asked.

My temper flared, and with blood roaring in my ears, I glared the man down. "Bummer isn't going anywhere but home with me," I said.

I dug in my front pocket for the bank envelope that held my withdrawal. "I'll take Gypsy too. Here's five hundred dollars in cash for both." I threw the envelope down where the man could reach it.

"No way, lady." He smirked, shaking his head. "It's not about the money. I won't rest until that horse is chopped up for dog food. I plan to tag along just so I can watch."

I returned his gaze coolly. "Well, then, we have a big problem. I won't rest until the humane society closes down this fire trap and cites you for every safety violation they can think of. Of course, that would be after I testify against you for cruel and inhumane treatment of these animals."

He paled at my words.

"Yeah," Sara piped in, standing behind me. "I'll help her. We saw you use that electric fence to hurt Bummer. I think you got exactly what you deserved."

The man looked from me to Sara and back again. "Fine, take them both," he said, throwing up his uninjured hand. "That horse will kill you."

As if Bummer wanted to make a bigger ass out of the man, the chestnut nuzzled my dark hair. Gently tugging the scrunchie that held the end of my long braid, he pulled the bright red material with his teeth. Once it came loose, he bounced his head up and down and twitched his lips, as if grinning. He stood calmly with it dangling from his mouth, snuffing quietly.

"Damn beast, I'll be happy to be rid of ya," the man muttered, as he hobbled into the barn.

I'm happy to report that Bummer and Gypsy are healthy and happy, and they love to go trail riding. Gypsy learned quickly and easily and is the sweetest horse any rider could hope for. Bummer is a character, and it took a bit longer for him to come around, but that's another story.

Cheri Jalbert

Back in the Saddle with Sundance

"Get away!" I scolded, waving my hands to shoo away the dogs. But Sparky and her near-grown puppies ignored me. They barked and nipped at Sundance's feet. Sensing trouble, I reached up to grab the bridle, but at that moment the pony bucked, snorted, and tossed his head. Instead of catching the leather, I caught only air. The pony bucked again, kicked at the dogs, and galloped away with my visually impaired daughter, Katy, on his back.

The shaggy pony and his captive rider charged straight toward the chicken enclosure. I ran across the slippery, wet grass chasing after them. *Oh, why wasn't I more careful?* I scolded myself.

Earlier, when that Saturday had dawned sunny after two days of rain, Katy had begged me to ride Joanne's pony. So I called my friend for permission.

"Sure, come on over," she said. "But I think you should ride in the backyard. The pasture is so muddy today."

That would have been a great idea—if Sundance hadn't noticed all that food in the chicken yard, and the dogs hadn't barked at him.

Now as I ran, I watched the pony tuck his head down and plow under the fence. The wire barbs scraped Katy's legs; she tried to avoid them by leaning further back in the saddle. Finally she leaned so far back that her head touched the pony's rump. The sharp wire ripped into her legs and gouged bloody stripes from her knee to neck. Katy cried, "Help me, Mommy! Ow! Help!" But my intrepid eight-year-old still clung to the saddle.

"I'm on my way," I yelled. "Hang on."

I had almost reached the pony when I slipped and fell. Now, my butt hurt, my left wrist felt bruised, and my pants were sopping wet. As I scrambled up again, I remembered how, seven months prior, Katy began riding here. I had invited my new friend, Joanne, for tea. When she came into our kitchen, Joanne noticed Katy hunched over her sketch book, drawing a rearing horse.

"Wow, your picture is gorgeous. I'll bet you really like horses, don't you?" Joanne had asked my daughter.

Lifting her head and squinting at Joanne, Katy nodded furiously. "I love horses. I wish I had one so I could ride it all the time."

"Maybe you could come and ride my pony, Sundance," Joanne offered. "My children are all grown up, and I think he's lonely."

Katy jumped up, almost tipping over her chair in her excitement. "Could I really? Oh, Mommy, can we go sometime to ride Joanne's pony?"

I chuckled at her enthusiasm. "I guess so."

After that, I had driven Katy to Joanne's two-acre "farm" to ride almost every Saturday. She had learned a lot about riding in that time. Katy and Sundance—a Welsh pony with a bit of quarter horse mixed in—became friends; I thought I could trust him. Obviously, my trust was premature.

Now, I rubbed my behind and started running again. When Sundance reached the chicken enclosure, he trampled the wire mesh that kept the hens contained. Chickens squawked and fluttered around the pony, through the hole he made in the wire, and into the grass beyond. Then the dogs joined the fun, chasing the chickens around the yard, into the pasture, and finally, out into the fields.

Katy screamed again, "Ow, ow! Help me!"

I stepped over barbed wire and scrambled through the razed enclosure toward my daughter. "I'm coming, honey." I heaved a huge piece of jagged wire out of my way and finally reached the pony, who, oblivious to Katy, dogs, hens, me, and the mayhem he had created, dropped his head and gobbled up chicken feed.

As I wrapped my scratched, dirty arms around Katy, she let go of the saddle horn, clamped her arms around my neck, and buried her face in my shoulder. When I lifted her down, her tears left dirty stains on my shirt. Then I helped Katy hobble through the wire mess and onto Joanne's porch, where we both sat down.

"That chin looks sore," I said, examining a big scrape there. "It doesn't need stitches, though. That's the good part. The rest of your scrapes look impressive, but they aren't deep either. Let's go inside and doctor you up."

Just then, Joanne stepped out of her sliding door onto the porch. "I heard Katy crying; I'm so sorry about this." She thrust a box of bandages into my hands. "Here, take these. I'll get the pony." She jogged down the steps toward Sundance and her now-destroyed chicken yard.

I led Katy into the house, where I washed and dressed her wounds. When we returned outside, Joanne had already removed Sundance's saddle and bridle and released him to the pasture and was back at the coop examining the damage.

I hugged Katy. "Stay here and rest, honey. I'll be back in a bit."

When I arrived at the destruction, I said, "Gee, Joanne, I feel really bad about this. How about letting me help pay for the repairs."

Tendrils of Joanne's long auburn hair blew in her face. She wiped her scratched and dirty palms on the front of her jeans and brushed her hair back with her hand. She shook her head. "No, I'm the one who told you to ride in the yard. I knew Sundance liked chicken feed. He's done this before, and I should have warned you. But I'll accept help putting it back together. Just let me get the hammer and some staples."

Joanne and I reconstructed the enclosure. Then we rounded up and deposited the chickens into it. Finally, I flopped down next to Katy on the porch. She had her knees tucked up to her chest and her arms wrapped around them. The band was falling out of her long brown hair, and the swollen, red scratches on her legs still oozed. Tears still streamed down her face. "I don't ever want to ride a pony again," she sobbed.

It had been an emotionally and physically difficult day, and I wasn't too crazy about bringing her to Joanne's to ride again, either. But I wanted to help her learn bravery. Katy was already afraid of so many things due to her visual impairment and the teasing she endured at school.

I nodded. "I understand. I remember how frightened I was to get back on when my pony bucked me off the first time." I paused a moment or two. "But Katy, if you don't ride him again, you might be afraid of ponies forever. And you love Sundance. He wasn't trying to hurt you. He was just hungry."

Katy was quiet a long while. At last she mumbled, "I can't ride him now, though."

"Okay. Let's just put away the saddle and bridle and come back when you're ready."

Katy seemed hesitant, but finally she nodded. "I guess I can touch his saddle."

Two weeks after the chicken coop disaster, Katy slid onto a chair in the kitchen for breakfast. "Mom, I think I want to ride again, but I'm scared. I'll go if you hold Sundance's bridle the whole time. Promise me." She poured a bowl of cereal.

I passed her the milk. "I promise."

When we arrived at Joanne's, I expected Katy to ride just a few moments. But to my surprise, she stayed on about twenty minutes. I held the bridle the whole time.

After that, we returned Saturday after Saturday. With each visit, Sundance became more responsive and Katy grew bolder. Eventually, she was willing to ride without me holding on again and even let the pony trot or canter.

One afternoon I sat on the wooden fence watching Katy prepare for her ride. She pulled a comb through Sundance's tough, wiry mane and then brushed him. When she finished, Katy rewarded the pony with a chunk of apple and patted his neck. Sundance nuzzled her and put his head down. Katy scratched behind his ears.

Then she squinted up at me. "Mom, I'll bet you don't know why I like riding so much, do you? Want to know what it feels like for me?"

I nodded. "Sure."

"I know I'll never be able to drive a car, 'cause I can't see well enough. But I can imagine how great that would feel—to go where I want, when I want, all by myself. That's how it feels to ride Sundance—free and fun."

With practiced precision, Katy picked up the saddle, set it on Sundance's back, and tightened the cinch. She slid the bit into the pony's mouth and slipped the bridle over his ears. Finally, Katy grabbed the saddle horn and swung onto her mount. Her motions seemed so natural and effortless they looked dance-like, even choreographed. And all the while, she spoke quiet endearments to her mount.

Once Katy was on Sundance, she squinted toward me and smiled. "But do you know why Sundance is much better than any car, Mom?"

I shook my head. "Tell me."

Katy patted the pony's neck again. "Because I love him and he loves me back. Thanks for making me ride again. I'm not afraid anymore."

She clicked her tongue and tapped the pony's ribs with her heels. Then she waved her hand in the air. As Sundance trotted away into the dusty field, girl and pony merged in motion. It was a good day.

Ellen Tomaszewski

My Chocolate-Coated Destiny

It began as a beautiful autumn day—almost magical in its warmth and color. When such a day blooms, I simply cannot allow it to pass without taking a ride. My only hesitation that fall day was who to take. My trusty Morgan, Cocoa, had just returned from spending the summer with a world champion reining stallion and had been confirmed in foal only twenty days before. So I decided, instead, to take not-so-trusty Sarru, a gorgeous, headstrong, old show horse who had never quite adapted to use on the trail. Though I used her often, especially during my own mare's absences, Sarru was not the dependable mount Cocoa was.

I entered the barn to a chorus of whinnies and nickers, took the halter from Sarru's door, and slipped it over the lovely head that reached out to me. I led her into the aisle and put her in the cross ties. While

I groomed her, my gaze drifted toward the rear of the barn, where a large point of white caught my eye. It was what I had dubbed Cocoa's "headlight"—her star, brilliant white against rich dark chestnut, often the only visible clue that a horse was standing in the shadows.

Cocoa watched intently as I readied Sarru. I spoke to my Morgan, and she nickered to me, but I continued to ready the larger mare. As I was hoisting the saddle to Sarru's broad back, I hesitated and my eyes again found the large white spot in the dark rear stall. To this day, I don't know what made me change my mind. In retrospect, I would have to say it was divine intervention coupled with the sheer force of will of a little chocolate mare who desperately wanted to be out on the trail after not being ridden for so long.

I pulled off the saddle, gave Sarru a piece of the carrot I had brought with me, and returned her to her stall. Then I walked down the aisle, entered Cocoa's stall, and received the kisses she gave me whenever I opened her door. Talking gently to her, I slipped on her halter and led her out to the cross ties. A horse of great character and comedic ability, she kept me amused with her antics as we tacked up. Soon I was in the saddle, and we were heading out to the woods.

Cocoa and I had developed a rapport that went beyond horse and owner. We were in sync; we were best friends.

I was an adult amateur—less than an amateur, since "amateur" implies some degree of knowledge or skill ride—when I had acquired Cocoa. I had always loved Morgans—perhaps they appealed to my artistic side—and had known from a young age that one day I would have one. It took me until I was in my thirties, but better late than never.

Cocoa was a dream come true. Armed only with advice from her breeder and a few riding lessons, I embarked on the adventure of training her myself—and what an adventure it was! While I was training her, I was also learning how to ride and drive. We learned together, and we faced all of our "firsts" together, including our first jump course, competing with horses literally twice her size. She placed fourth. Next time, she pranced away with the blue—obviously quite pleased with her accomplishment, leaving all the other riders seated on their big Thoroughbreds and Warmbloods, gaping after the classy little 14-hand Morgan who had bested them at her, and my, second jump course ever.

We showed, we trail rode, we gamed, we jumped, and we did English and Western pleasure. We joined the American Morgan Horse Association's (AMHA)

Pathways Program and signed up for the Open Competition Program, eventually earning our bronze medal for show and placing a respectable fifth in the general category in 2000.

Basically, because the Morgan world was so new to me and I wanted to dive into it, I embraced all things Morgan—even winning the AMHA photography contest once and the art competition three times. Inspired by the Pathways Program's trail notes, I began chronicling my experiences with my Morgan in a journal and adapting them into stories for publication.

Of all the firsts and good times Cocoa and I had shared, we enjoyed the trails the most. Cocoa was happiest trail riding or pleasure driving, and it had become a form of meditation for both of us. She was an intuitive, intelligent, and consistently dependable mount. Her alert carriage and composure in the face of just about anything—including a brush fire once—made her an invaluable trail companion. In fact, the noise and confusion of sirens, fire trucks, and firemen had left her unfazed; the only thing that upset her about that occasion was being put in her stall, where she couldn't see the action! Many years later, some firemen still ask about the courageous little chocolate mare that came out of the smoke that day.

Our leisurely ride that gentle autumn afternoon began as nice and easy as always. We wandered through fields and into a wood belonging to a neighbor, completely at ease and thoroughly enjoying the day and each other's company.

Along one of the well-traveled trails that snaked through a bog, one that I had trotted Sarru on just the day before, Cocoa took what I assumed was a simple misstep. She recovered immediately, so I didn't think much of it—until she stopped and dove at her right front leg, at the same time making a small leap. I was a bit confused by her behavior, but not overly concerned. Then something hit me in the back of the neck, and I struck at it reflexively. This caused me to pitch a little in the saddle, and Cocoa again dropped her head to her legs.

Still not sure what was happening, I tried to urge her on and get out of there, but she only knew something was hurting her and was busy addressing that, not immediately paying attention to my heels. So I attempted to make an emergency dismount so I could lead her out of there—just as she gave a mighty buck of frustration, and I fell instead of landing on my feet. Somehow, my foot got tangled in the stirrup leather, the iron acting like a grappling hook and keeping it tightly wrapped around my ankle. I even lost the reins in the fray. As I sat in the dirt, dangling from the side of my horse by one leg, I noticed a loud buzzing sound and saw a black cloud rising and swirling around me—hornets!

Cocoa's hoof had gone through a hornet's nest in the ground, and now I was looking up at a horse hovering on the brink of insanity, with my foot still caught in the stirrup and with several large trees surrounding us, while a swarm of irate hornets attacked us. Certain I would soon be wrapped around one of those trees, I strained to reach the offending stirrup leather as Cocoa wheeled around, obviously intending to bolt for home as fast as she could. But in the moment she began her spin, a strange thing happened: Her large, expressive eyes met mine, and I saw a flicker in them—a comprehension that I was in deep trouble down there.

To my astonishment, in spite of the pain she was enduring and heedless of the fear, that little mare ceased her movements almost completely, doing nothing more than tossing her head in her intense discomfort. I managed to say "Whoa!" a few times, but I had no physical control over her at that point. In the face of what was happening, I am amazed she complied at all. Not only did she stand still while I got the cursed leather unwrapped from my leg, she also waited to move until I was up, had the reins over her head, and told her to run with me. A half mile later, we were still picking hornets out of our manes! The entire incident probably lasted only a minute or so, but it was one of the longest moments of my life!

We were more than a mile from home, and both of us were badly stung. When Cocoa began to sweat profusely, I became deeply concerned that she was having an allergic reaction or that the incident might cause her to slip her foal. Meanwhile, I praised and reassured her as we walked, running concerned hands over her bumpy body and thanking her for her cool head and intelligence in the face of all that pain and mayhem. She gave me the impression that my fussing was completely unnecessary. To her, she had done what any good horse would do for her human, and while I was fretting about her, she was stopping every few minutes to nose me over. Still, the more I praised her, the higher her head rose. Her face shone with that regal Morgan look, and I could see in her eyes the ghosts of all her noble forebears—right back to Figure himself, just twelve generations past.

A little antihistamine, a good rubdown, and an apple-and-carrot medley upon our arrival home, and Cocoa was up to her old tricks of "smiling" for her reward of laughter and giving of kisses. We both were covered in welts and uncomfortable for many days, but otherwise, we were physically unscathed.

Unfortunately, we lost the new life growing within her, due to the venom of the many stings Cocoa suffered while she stood stone-still until I was safely on my feet. I was never able to successfully breed her again, so she will remain a unique gem—forever one of a kind and cherished for all my days.

I have little doubt that if I had ignored the impulse to take Cocoa out that day and if Sarru had been the one to step into that hornet's nest, Sarru would have panicked and seriously injured or killed me. Once again, my amazing mare had proven her connection with and devotion to me. I am truly blessed to have in my life this noble Morgan—my Heritage Royal Destiny, my Cocoa.

Heather Mitchell

A Man's Best Friend

January's frosty white light was fading fast as we drove west toward the barn. It was almost five o'clock, and we didn't want to be late for my son's therapeutic horseback riding lesson. Nick has autism, which can often mean rigidity where timelines are concerned. Today was different, though; the lesson was at a new barn, with a new teacher. The riding organization had recently undergone some changes. The stress of all that newness made Nick very nervous. To top it all off, it was Nick's eighteenth birthday.

At least the horse would be the same—old Cheyenne. He was a lively, chestnut Morgan, a solid powerhouse of easygoing willingness. His soft brown eyes spoke patience, and he had much more to offer than just a ride. Nick was twelve years old when he first met Cheyenne and in desperate need of a friend.

Autism can cause social isolation. By the time a child with autism hits adolescence, the nuances of social interaction between peers can become impossible to navigate. Unlike with younger children, play dates get harder and harder to set up, and opportunities for friendships can shrink.

When Nick neared junior high, I decided it was critical to find some sort of extra-curricular activity for him. He needed something that would challenge him physically and that offered him an emotional as well as a social outlet. It certainly wouldn't hurt if it was fun too. As luck would have it, I ran into another mother of a child with autism who told me about a therapeutic horseback riding program for children with a variety of disabilities. I wasted no time in signing Nick up.

The moment he rode Cheyenne, that was it. He tried out two other horses at the stable, but it was Cheyenne that Nick bonded tightly with.

At the beginning of the lessons Nick had trouble following the directions of the instructor. He would often get frustrated or angry, at times having to get off the horse and end the lesson before his hour was up. Slowly, Nick learned how to saddle and bridle Cheyenne, how to lead him over to the ramp and mount, and how to unsaddle him and brush his coat to a fine sheen. Once Nick learned to trot and canter, he was never satisfied with a slow walk and he and Cheyenne could be seen trotting around the corral every Monday afternoon.

The rhythm of the horse, the sensory input, put a smile on Nick's face, no matter how badly the day had gone. The weeks turned into months and then years. Nick went from junior high to high school, and during that time the challenges became so much for him he had to drop down to a half a day of school. Still, every Monday he could depend on his good friend, Cheyenne, to be there for him. Cheyenne didn't seem to care that Nick had autism, and Nick never minded that his best friend had four legs.

Of course, as Nick was growing up, Cheyenne was aging, too. Some days he moved a little slower. Still, the trainers commented how he seemed to perk up when Nick showed up. Even on days when Cheyenne had been acting tired, when Nick hopped on him, the horse was always up for a swift canter around the corral.

Trail rides added a layer of adventure to their friendship. Over the years, I followed Nick and Cheyenne on trail rides on summer days, smelling wild chamomile and pennyroyal as it was crushed under the horses' hooves. In the fall, we rode near the river, where cottonwood trees shed their pollen like snow. The highlight of the year was an overnight trip, when all the riders camped out near the beach and were able to gallop the horses along the shore. Nick found caring companionship, not only with Cheyenne, but also with other riders and his trusted teachers, Lonna and Julie.

Through all those Mondays, Cheyenne remained a loyal friend. As we drove to the barn on the cold January day of Nick's eighteenth birthday, we expected nothing different.

We parked our car and went to the stables. We saw several other horses, but no Cheyenne.

The new teacher came up to us and said unceremoniously, "Didn't someone call you? Cheyenne has retired. He's at the old barn. What horse would you like to ride instead?"

I knew my son would not understand—and, indeed, he did not. For a brief minute, I thought there might be a meltdown. I leaned over to him and calmly said, "If you don't want to ride today, that's okay. We can go talk about it in the car." He nodded.

The old barn was only a few miles away. There was no question that we would drive straight there. My son was in tears, not ready for this sudden end to his most trusted friendship. I was afraid he would be inconsolable, worrying over what to say to help him through this unexpected blow, when suddenly I found the words that needed to be said.

"Cheyenne waited for you. He knows you are a man and that you will be okay. He is a very old horse and very tired. Maybe he just needs to take it easy."

My son took a deep breath and looked at me from tear-filled eyes. His look told me he knew in his heart that this was true. If it had happened on any other day, I'm sure the transition would have been next to impossible. But because it happened on Nick's eighteenth birthday, it made sense to him.

We stopped at the old barn to say goodbye to Cheyenne. His owner apologized profusely, and explained that the change had been abrupt and could not be helped. She told us where Cheyenne's new home would be—a barn near the sea, with lots of pasture where he could roam freely. She added that we could visit him anytime.

I gave Nick all the time he needed with Cheyenne, to say goodbye. I could hear him explaining to the horse, very much like he would a person, that he'd become a man and would find some new friends. And he thanked him for being his best friend—when no one else knew how.

Elizabeth King Gerlach

Horse on Lap

Sugar was supposed to be my dream horse, but so far she'd been a white nightmare.

"You crazy horse," I chided her when she balked at the sight of a charred cedar post in the fence line. "You've been past that blackened pole before, and it hasn't changed a bit. And it doesn't have ghosts."

Sugar snorted and sidestepped, and it felt like I was sitting atop an earthquake. Putting pressure on her ribs with my heel, I encouraged her to walk over to inspect the post. Her muscular body tensed—her ears pricked forward and her neck arched in the bow shape that makes Arabians so beautiful—and she refused to budge.

Heaving a sigh of defeat, I gathered the reins in one hand and slid out of the saddle. The dust from my jeans rose in puffs as I swatted them clean and then stretched my tired back. The fragrance of horse and leather drifted past me, but I was too mad to enjoy it. "If there was a glue factory around here, you would be a bottle of Elmer's right now," I threatened.

Apparently, Sugar had heard that line before. She turned her back to the fence pole without so much as a crow hop and walked sedately behind me.

"Oh yeah, now all of a sudden you're not worried about the screaming meemies that live in that post."

It wasn't the first time a pleasure ride had ended this way—with me walking half-heartedly back to the corral and with Sugar trailing behind, as happy as a June bug in a saddle blanket because she had managed to get me off her back.

A few days earlier, I rode her bareback in the half-acre at the back of the house, and she plodded along as if she were a pack mule instead of an Arabian. Finally, after a considerable amount of nagging encouragement, she started trotting. I bounced around, wondering how a horse could be so broad and so bony at the same time. My neck felt like a Slinky that had come uncoiled, and I wondered if I were getting whiplash in the process.

She finally broke into a smooth gallop, and just as I was about to shout "Wahoo!"—she hit the brakes. The ground and I had a sudden, unplanned meeting. I limped back to the corral, worried the hip

I'd landed on had cracked like an old plate. Sugar meandered behind, complacently mouthing the bit and probably laughing the whole way.

Oh sure, Sugar loved me. Loved for me to feed her a can of sweet, crunchy oats. To shoo the pesky flies away from her chocolate-brown eyes. To gently curry her broad back and silver-white mane and tail until she glistened. But to ride her? No way. To have a spiritual connection? Never.

The sky slowly shifted from spring blue to creek-water gray, and the temperature dropped as I tied up Sugar and took off the bridle. She exhaled as I slid the saddle off her back and the clovery scent of hay billowed past me in a puff.

I've always loved horses, and as a child of the sixties living in the suburbs, I had dreamed of owning one. I'd watched *Fury* and *My Friend Flicka*, and worshipped Roy Rogers and Trigger. My memorabilia even included an autographed picture of Roy waving at the camera, while Trigger, the world's most magnificent palomino stallion, reared in the air.

So what was I doing wrong? Why didn't Sugar like me?

Fat drops of rain splattered on the saddle in my arms. I hustled into the shed to put it away. Grabbing a brush, I scrambled out and started cleaning the sweat and loose hair off Sugar. She turned her finely chiseled head and watched me, but only for a second. She rarely held eye contact for long.

As I finished brushing her, the rain began to drizzle. I climbed up on top of the corral, hooked my scuffed boots under the second rail, and sat for a minute in the cool, misty breeze. Sugar turned her back to me, but I was so used to being ignored by her that I didn't pay much attention at first.

Slowly, an inch at a time, she backed up.

"What is she doing?" I asked my husband, Russ, who had come out and climbed up on the top rail to sit with me.

"I don't know, but if she gets much closer, you'll be crushed by horse butt," he replied.

A wiser woman would probably have jumped out of the way, but I was too fascinated by her behavior to give up my ringside seat.

Another slow step closer. I could see the tiny droplets of rainwater on her hair and smell the sweat on her hide.

Another step closer. The heat from her hindquarters radiated toward my legs, warming them in the chilly air.

Another step closer. Sugar and I were now touching.

Then she picked up one hind leg and shifted her weight lightly onto my thighs. Russ and I stared.

Inside, I was cheering, but I held as still as a setter that has pointed a pheasant, my eyes round with surprise and my breathing shallow so as not to break the magic of the moment. My childhood hero might have had a horse that could rear and paw the air, but I had a horse sitting on my lap. All I could say was, "Let's see you top that, Roy."

Maybe Sugar did get spooked by nearly every twig and leaf. And maybe she did ignore my requests sometimes. So what? All that mattered was that my horse and I had made a connection.

C. L. Beck

A Pet Theory

My friend Vivienne and I shivered in the freezing cold barn, getting our horses ready to hunt.

"I don't care, Vivi. I've got a perfect attendance record for the year." I bent down and cleaned out the last of my horse's hooves. "Besides, if I keep a perfect attendance record, maybe I'll get my colors this year. You know how much I want that award."

She shook her head and cast a quizzical glance at my horse. "Well, it should be an interesting hunt. I can't believe you're actually riding him."

"Him" was a four-year-old Thoroughbred gelding named Peace Train. Yep, after the song. He had several pet names, too, some quite colorful.

We finished tacking up the horses and threw on their heavy winter blankets, adjusting the side straps under their bellies.

I had hooked up the trailer earlier that morning, and now the truck idled in the driveway. Puffs of gray exhaust came out of the tail pipe as the cold engine warmed. The horses loaded easily, and we headed down the road.

The hunt club was just a little over a mile away. Most of the time we hacked over, but the ominous sky threatened rain, and we didn't want to ride home in a storm. In addition, I was riding a young horse, one that was not exactly crazy about jumping. Actually, he'd developed quite a stop, and I was fast losing patience with him.

I had long held to the theory that the hunt field was an excellent place to teach a green horse to go forward to the fences. I'd just never had the opportunity to give it a try. Until today. My premise was that a horse, because of its herd instinct, will do almost anything to keep up with the field. I would be riding the perfect horse to test out the veracity of that idea.

Plus, given the fact that my mare, Goldy, had just thrown a shoe, it was hunt Peace or not hunt at all. That, of course, was out of the question.

As we drove down the driveway to the hunt club, I noticed the other riders had already mounted. Peace was an impatient sort, partly due to his age, and I didn't want to hang around while the huntsman called hounds from the kennels and got everybody sorted out.

We parked the trailer under some trees and unloaded the horses. Trembling with excitement, Peace neighed, loud and long. Several other horses replied, getting him even more wound up. As I mounted, I felt his body tremble in fear and anticipation. He'd never seen so many horses before, and his ears pricked high, almost touching. We horsepeople all know what happens when horse ears touch: instant insanity!

Peace danced in place, eager to approach the strange group of horses, but still holding back, reticent and unsure of himself. At four, he still felt inferior to other adult horses and had retained the annoying foal habit of chewing, thus showing his submission. Frothy foam covering his muzzle, he chewed like crazy at the approaching field. I walked him in a circle under the tree, trying to settle him, as the riders grouped together.

Vivienne waved goodbye as she joined the main field, a quizzical look on her face. She flashed me the victory sign and grinned.

I would ride last in line. If my theory proved false, at least I wouldn't hold up the rest of the field.

We crossed the frozen pasture and started up the road at a trot. Peace rolled into his long, ground-covering strides. Several times I had to turn up a driveway so the field could move ahead. Then we'd play the catch-up game.

We'd barely made it into the meadow when hounds hit a hot line. I looked across the field just in time to see the fox streaking into the woods. The huntsman blew "Gone Away" as hounds took off on the line.

Well, Peace nearly blew a gasket. The field thundered after the pack, jumping a very nice, inviting little panel that crossed the trail. I kept circling, and Peace kept bucking, little bucks, but bucks all the same, until the entire field had jumped over the panel.

I followed the last horse in line, about six strides back. Peace saw the fence coming up, and by the swiveling of his ears, I knew he was doing a lot of thinking. I felt him begin to shorten his stride, and thought, *Okay, here goes with the theory.* I just sat there, chilly.

He stopped dead in front of the fence, quivering. I waited him out. He pawed the ground several times, aiming shrill neighs at the departing field. I circled him away from the fence, preparing to give it another try. He caught sight of the field as it ascended the far hill and made a decision. When I turned him back toward the fence, I just sat quiet again, doing nothing.

It had to be his choice. He maintained his pace, got the perfect spot, and sailed over. All on his own.

Before long we closed the distance to the field. We climbed the steep hill at a gallop, both of us quite out of breath when we reached the top. Down in the valley we saw hounds being recast. The welcome break allowed us to catch our breath. I kept Peace well back of the field, but the last gallop had taken a bit of the starch out of him, so he behaved well, waiting for my next signal.

Suddenly, two hounds spoke in unison, and every horse in the field drew a bead on the sound, heads up, tails raised like flags. The huntsman blew "Gone Away" again.

We all surged to life, falling in behind the field master, whose horse took off like a shot, pursuing the racing hounds. The field, strung out now in single file, approached a stone wall. It provided the only access into the next field. The rugged gray wall, solid and thick, looked formidable. I wasn't sure how Peace would react to test two.

We stayed behind, last again, and I felt new confidence in my horse's stride. No doubt about it, this time he was going to go. I got a great lead from the horse ahead of me, and Peace sailed over the wall like a made hunter.

I knew if we continued in our present direction, we would encounter a serious test of my horse's newly acquired courage. Ahead lay a dirt road with a fairly high stock fence on both sides. There was no other way around. Either we jumped or we stopped hunting.

Joe, our huntsman, sent hounds on down the line, hoping to pick up the scent again. The field held up at the bottom of the slope as hounds recast. When the hounds hit the scent again, they took off, streaking up the slope, scrambling over rocks and fallen trees in hot pursuit of old Reynard.

The fox, obviously playing with the hounds, sat at the top of the hill, grinning. As the hounds spoke, he rose from his haunches and trotted into the underbrush.

Below him, the frantic hounds raced up the knoll.

I circled again, waiting for the rest of the field to go ahead. Peace got madder by the moment as I held him back. I knew he would need to be moving right along if he was going to clear both fences, and I didn't want to get caught between the two of them. That would give us a very close, very tight approach, impossible for a horse with no experience.

Well, I shouldn't have worried about that, because when I finally released Peace, he shot up the slope, looked at the fence and the disappearing field, and went for it. The second fence, only three strides away, came up so quickly he didn't have time to think about it. We tore after the field, and I laughed with joy. I knew it!

We kept up with the hunt from that point on, and Peace never stopped at a fence again—not in the hunt field, not in the show ring, and many times, not in the pasture. One fence got to looking pretty much like another to him, and any time he got bored, he'd hop out and go exploring. It made for lots of interesting forays around the neighborhood, but Peace never refused a fence again. Never.

Gayle Farmer

An Angel Called Amos

"The heart catherization shows severe blockage, 70 to 95 percent in two arteries, and most of the others are more than seventy percent blocked," the doctor said.

Within a week, Barry was undergoing quintuple bypass surgery.

At the hospital, I sat in a crowded waiting room with my family as doctors opened my husband's chest and repaired his heart. I would not let myself even think of life without my dearest friend.

Six hours later, the surgeon, still wearing his green cap and with his mask hanging from his neck, approached me. "He came through very well. He's in the intensive care unit. We'll watch him for a while before transferring him to a room. The next few months he'll need you to take care of him." Dr. Roberts smiled. "He is hard-headed, so you'll have to try to keep him from doing anything to set him back. I'll have the nurse give you some information for him to read when he gets home. Go on in and see him. He's on a respirator and can't talk, but he'll know you're there."

Tears of joy and relief wet my cheeks. I wanted to rush in, to be sure he was okay, but part of me was afraid. Barry had never been seriously ill, and I couldn't help but feel apprehensive about what was in store for both of us in the coming months.

Five days after his surgery, I brought Barry home to the farm. Walking as if he might break open at any moment, he moved from room to room, never without his pillow clutched to his chest to modify the sharp pain brought on by the slightest cough or sneeze.

Although Barry did not mention it, I knew he was thinking of his dad who had died from an embolism soon after undergoing surgery. Barry, like his father, had been smoking three packs of cigarettes a day when the heart attack occurred.

Having always been an active person—a golfer, water skier, and hiker—it was not in Barry's nature to sit inside the house and read, and he had no interest in day-time television. He had taught me, the more sedentary type, to ride dirt bikes and play tennis with him. Now, as prescribed, he walked a mile every day, gave up cigarettes, began a heart-healthy diet . . . and became more miserable with each passing hour.

Sometimes I'd glance across the room and see Barry wipe tears from his eyes. This was not the man I knew.

"What's wrong, honey?" I would ask him.

He would turn away, trying to hide this unfamiliar feeling he didn't understand.

My stalwart husband who always saw the glass half full, who picked me up when I was in the dumps and comforted me in times of sadness, was slipping into a well of darkness.

"Would you like to see a movie?" I'd ask. "Do you want me to invite someone over?"

He'd look at me with sad eyes and shake his head.

I read everything I could find on heart problems and open-heart surgery. The literature said heart patients often develop depression after surgery. I could understand how a vibrant man might feel, knowing his heart was damaged, wondering if he would ever be the same. I wanted to call his doctor, but I knew that Barry, being the kind of man who had always handled his own problems, would not discuss his feelings with anyone. I think he was afraid of showing his emotions, thinking it was a sign of weakness.

One day as he stood and watched me brush my little mare, he said, "I want another horse."

"Don't you think you're rushing things? Why not wait until you've healed some to start riding?" I asked, worried that he was in too much of a hurry to become active. A strange horse could be dangerous for someone in his fragile condition. It takes time to learn the personality of a new horse, to know what sets him off or how he might act in any given situation. I knew Barry was aware of that too.

But having been married to this man for twenty-four years, I knew that the passive lifestyle he was being forced to live was not good. Still, I was surprised to come home a few days later to find Amos standing in our yard.

"I told Chris I'd like to keep him for awhile and see if he works out for me," Barry said. "I certainly don't want a fast or flashy horse right now, but I think this one might be okay. Chris was happy to have me feed the old guy, and if I decide I want to keep him, I can."

Amos would not be the first horse to catch your eye if you came upon him in a herd. He had no fire in his eyes, and no famous blood ran through his veins. The slight sway in his back indicated he had been ridden a number of miles and was long in the tooth. But Barry said there was something special about Amos. He'd noticed it right away as he watched the tall chestnut gelding grazing amidst a few other steeds. Amos had raised his head at Barry's approach and stood quietly, not moving a muscle, except to switch his long tail occasionally to keep away the flies. "He seemed like he was waiting for me."

The horse trader, my nephew, was honest. "I've sold this horse three or four times in the past few years. He always comes back, but it's usually because the owner wants a more spirited, speedier horse, not because of anything Amos has done wrong."

Barry had ridden and owned other horses, but for several years his work had required him to travel around the country for several days each week. When he was home on weekends, he spent his leisure time on the golf course. We had sold his last horse after it became obvious he never had time to ride anymore.

Now, looking at big red Amos, fear tightened my throat. I thought of the possibility of my beloved husband being thrown and injured out on a trail somewhere. But then I saw a smile light Barry's face, and I couldn't help but feel better. That smile was brighter than the sun reflecting off the silver conchos on the horse's saddle. It was the first sign of happiness I'd seen in my husband in weeks.

Barry gingerly climbed aboard the gentle horse, who stood stone-still until his rider was settled and ready to go. When Barry lifted the reins, Amos stepped out slowly across the grass and down the farm road as though an inexperienced child sat upon his back. My heart filled, and so did my eyes.

In the weeks that followed, I noticed a change in Barry—a good change this time. He had a reason now to get up and get dressed each morning. His buddy waited in his stall and snuffled softly when Barry arrived to dump a bucket of grain into the trough. Most of that fall, the recuperating patient filled his time grooming his gelding or riding him among the fallen leaves in the woods. On those quiet rides, he had time to sort out his thoughts, to reflect on his life, and to appreciate the blessing of having another chance.

I was thankful for Amos. Having grown up with horses, I recognized that this giant animal was steady and unflappable. I was confident he would not bolt at an unusual noise or unexpected movement of ground birds. He was not strong-headed or stubborn and could be guided with a slight hand motion on the reins.

Like a dark cloud on the horizon dissipates as it rains out, Barry's depression faded. The sad and reclusive man departed, and my optimistic and fun-loving husband returned. He laughed more and teased me like he used to, and often, from another room, I'd hear him strumming his guitar and singing. In a few months, Barry's body and mind were healed, and he went back to work.

In my life, I've found that angels show up when we most need them, and not all of them wear flowing robes and wings. Some of them have flowing manes, four hooves, and big brown eyes that see deep into our broken hearts.

Glenda C. Beall

Mrs. Bladic's Mare

Mrs. Bladic, my father's client, was a short, Ukrainian woman of better-than-middle age. Excluding her voluminous bosom, she most resembled a good-natured Roberto "Hands of Stone" Duran, the Panamanian middleweight.

She met us in the farmyard, holding the reins of Dolly's new bridle. In the other hand swung a black vinyl handbag. Mrs. B. was always meticulously neat about her person. Her make-up was applied with a generous but accurate hand. Her pale blue babushka, pressed and spotless, surmounted an elaborate collection of metal curlers, bobby pins, and tissues. But of all Mrs. B.'s unique sartorial style, her most characteristic feature was her black vinyl handbag. Churchill had his cigar, Dirty Harry had a .45 Magnum, and Mrs. Bladic had a black vinyl handbag the size of a satchel.

Mrs. Bladic believed Dolly to be a capable jumper, based upon her capacity to clear the paddock fence bordering Mrs. B.'s vegetable garden. It was decided that Dolly must demonstrate her talent at the Victoria Day Horseshow. Having first purchased a complete and expensive set of tack, mail order from Birts Saddlery, Winnipeg, Mrs. B.'s next requirement was a jockey.

I was enchanted by the enormity of the mare. Beside her, I stood in roughly the proportion of a grown man to a dinosaur. The sun shone in pools on the expansive ebony hide in blue and purple highlights. Dolly was completely outfitted in her spotless new saddle, full bridle, and martingale, all in bright yellow London leather. It was hard to keep my feet as she nuzzled me for treats. The top of my head barely passed Dolly's huge, flat knees.

"Vell, dokter, what you tink, eh?"

"She's splendid," said my father.

"She can yump, by Gott," declared Mrs. Bladic.

My father left on his rounds.

"Okay, vee start. Kom on you," said Mrs. Bladic.

But first I needed to mount Dolly. A leg-up was out of the question, as Mrs. B. was not a tall person herself. It seemed that this wonderful project was in jeopardy at the outset. What we needed was a stepladder, but none was handy.

Mrs. Bladic looked about for some kind of elevating device. Her eyes fell upon a stout old poplar in spring blossom. "Dar," she pointed to the pale yellow tree.

I shinnied up to a convenient branch horizontal to the ground. Mrs. B. backed Dolly under it. It was a perfect fit. I slipped around the limb and landed lightly in the saddle, while Dolly stood like a statue waiting for her next direction.

"Goot, goot!" crowed Mrs. B. "Ve begin."

Perched atop that saddle, I must have looked like a blond peanut on an ebony mountain.

Our training facilities were basic, involving the lane of a cow path bordered by two rows of red alders. At one end of the lane were five sliding bars in a barbed wire fence line. That would serve as our practice jump. Mrs. B. stood by this gate with all but one rail removed, presenting to Dolly and me a formidable 18 inches of jump.

"Gallump! Gallump!" cried Mrs. B., by way of technical advice.

I turned Dolly around at the far end of the path. My legs didn't quite pass the horizontal arc of her belly, but I kicked on nevertheless. I kicked; I clucked; I gyrated about. Through the stiff new flaps of the saddle and the generous layer of fat covering her sides, Dolly could not have felt my legs at all. But like most draft horses, Dolly was amiable.

She agreed to break into a gentle trot. She sedately approached the "fence." All 18 inches loomed before us. She jumped. Seventeen hands and 1,900 pounds were briefly airborne. Though little experienced in any form of equitation, I had a sense of self-preservation. I dropped the reins on her neck and grabbed a double fistful of Dolly's luxuriant mane. It was magic. She was a huge, maternal Pegasus. Mrs. B. clapped with enthusiasm. The black, vinyl bag, the strap cradled in the crook of her elbow, bobbed and jumped.

After having enlarged the obstacle with the addition of a rail, Mrs. B. again exhorted me to "Gallump, gallump, you!" In spite of all my efforts, I could not stir Dolly beyond a rolling trot. Several training sessions later, it was decided that, certain shortcomings aside, notably the absence of any "gallumping," Dolly and I were ready for the Victoria Day Show.

The day dawned with all the ethereal charm of spring in Northwestern Ontario. My father delivered me early that morning to the Bladic place, and I helped groom and load Dolly on the old stock truck. The box was open on top, so Dolly's wise head could be seen over the cab, a yellow ribbon plaited neatly into her forelock waving in the breeze. She shone. From the mobile tips of her jet-black ears to the end of her wavy shampooed tail, she exuded health and well-being.

I climbed into the old rig next to Mr. Bladic and beside Mrs. B., who was to drive. Rosary beads, a crucifix, and a large set of fluffy dice hung from the rearview mirror. In terms of nonmaterial supports, we were well covered. The truck roared to life, and we were off, up and down the steep hills of Dog Lake Road, the gears whining in protest. A marvellously satisfying aroma of Mr. Bladic's pipe tobacco mixed with Mrs. Bladic's flowery cologne filled the cab.

Bumping through the gates of the fairgrounds, Dolly nickered. The show was mixed in character, quite an anachronism by today's standards. Driving classes and quarter horse reining events were interspersed with hunters under saddle and children's mounted games. The jumping classes were always saved to the end of the day. A course of small jumps was erected by the Lakehead Light Horse Association for the Junior Jumping Class.

A group of kids mounted on ponies of various types assembled for the contest. I was somewhat conspicuous, because most of the ponies did not reach the height of Dolly's ample belly. The eccentric appearance of Dolly in her brand new tack, accompanied by our intrepid coach, elicited snickers from some of the more upscale kids. Vanity and an inflated sense of one's social prominence can be two of the less-desirable qualities of equestrian neophytes.

But horses and, more particularly, ponies, have a way of returning a child to the harsher realities of life. There were red faces and tears beneath the black velvet hard hats as each child failed to negotiate the course without a penalty.

My turn came. Dolly walked into the ring with all the decorum and dignity of the good Queen herself. She circled, breaking into a slow, stately trot. We approached the first jump, a small white brush box filled with cedar. "Gallump, gallump!" called out Mrs. B. from the rail. I tried hard to carry out her instruction. I leaned forward. I clucked. I squeezed. But Dolly remained unperturbed; down one side of the ring she trotted, clearing each jump with purposeful, if ponderous, regularity. Turning at the bottom, we prepared to come up the other side. The last two jumps to be taken were big by the standards of our preparation, fully three feet high. It seemed doubtful that a mare of such mammoth proportions could project herself far enough into the air to clear the obstacles, going at such a modest pace.

I could see Mrs. B. at the far end of the row of jumps, and I knew what she was thinking. Dolly must "gallump" if we were to have any chance of getting to the end of the course. Mrs. Bladic, however, was equal to every contingency. From the recesses of the vinyl bag appeared, in her hands, a tin pail full of oats. Just as I commenced my final line of jumps, Mrs. B. tilted the pail toward us and banged the tin with a ladle. Dolly pricked her ears, and then a miracle—she broke into a round, slow canter. What delight! The easy sway of her motion was intoxicating; on she came, clearing the barriers with style.

How could we ever have doubted her? I was elated. Mrs. B. and her family—namely, Mr. B., the two grown boys, and Erma, their daughter—were ecstatic. They cheered without restraint. From my position on her back, I clasped Dolly's huge neck and squeezed as hard as I could. We won! The Bladic family crowded around us, hugging and patting their wonderful mare. Dolly accepted the adoration of her connections with her usual grace . . . more interested in her treat.

Our pleasure was short-lived. Could the use of oats be construed as unauthorized assistance? An indignant parent of one of my competitors had lodged a complaint. Mrs. B. confronted the judge as we stood arrayed behind her. The silver clasp of her black vinyl bag glinted in the sunshine. Her expression was stern.

"Zo, no vair, eh?"

Two beads of perspiration appeared on the receding forehead of the judge. "My dear Mrs. Bladic," he began, "it seems . . . someone feels . . . it's a question of the oats . . ."

"Zo, zumone veels, do day? Vel, Mr. Joodge . . ." At which point Mrs. B. reopened her bag. It was large enough to contain many items. An instrument of coercion might well have been concealed in its depths. All was quiet. The judge took an involuntary step to the rear. Mrs. B. reached slowly into the deep bag. Situated between her powder compact, her bright red lipstick, and a purse-size Harlequin Romance #73 was a small, thick book entitled *The Rules of the Canadian Horse Shows Association*. Withdrawing the little volume and pointing it at the judge, she said, "I 'ave 'ear de rules. Days nootin' 'gainst oats."

The judge was relieved. "But of course, if you have a copy of the rules . . ."

Mrs. B. hung Dolly's red rosette beside the rosary, crucifix, and the fluffy dice, where it remained for the life of the truck. It was late afternoon. A golden light bathed the interior of the old rig. We loaded Dolly for the return journey, and Mrs. B. let out the clutch.

When the truck pulled off the highway on to Dog Lake Road, Mrs. Bladic spoke, "You vill 'ave zum zupper, you." There were thick roast beef sandwiches with hot mustard, spicy pickles, raspberry pie, and iced tea in the kitchen.

John C. Hobson

Track Tales

B W Baryshnikov, or "Nick" as we called him, was an Arabian race horse. Though he was a great runner and a stakes winner with a show champion sire, he was also a gelding and always ran in the shadow of his maternal half-brother, BW Rasputin+/, a stallion and also a great runner. Perhaps that second-hand status is why Nick was such a character and had such an attitude. Of course, giving up the family jewels enabled him to have a meaningful career, just as it did the many Kelsos, Funny Cides, and John Henrys. But there was trial by fire, and trial by water, and trial by Baryshnikov.

To set the stage for this story, I must tell you how it was in those early years when Arabian racing was in its infancy. Nick won his first start at a little bush track in Idaho, where the track announcer

mispronounced his name, calling him "Berryskinoff."
No wonder Nick developed an attitude!

My Arabians have always suffered from what I
have come to call the "me syndrome": "Me first,"
"Me too," "Notice me," "What about me," "Take care
of me," etc. Baryshnikov just had more pronounced
symptoms of this affliction. And I, of course, totally
amused and entertained by his antics, unwittingly
reinforced and encouraged his questionable behavior
all along the way.

After Baryshnikov's first few races, he could no
longer be "ponied" during the post parade in the traditional manner, where the race horse is led by a rider
mounted on what we call a "pony horse." Instead, his
escort was instructed to just accompany him, hands
off and at a safe distance, because he enjoyed savag-
ing the pony horses, even those outweighing him
by several hundred pounds. And sometimes these
attacks would also include the pony riders. They all
began to think that Nick was the stallion, and this,
no doubt, pleased him. Being unencumbered by a
lead line gave Nick the opportunity to demonstrate
his animated park horse trot in the post parade.
Rarely was his jockey pleased, however.

His first trip to the test barn for the traditional
winner's urine test was uneventful. But that first,

small track didn't have a real test barn—just some portable panels set up in a well-lighted livestock pavilion. His next two wins came at Harbor Park and Yakima Meadows, where there were real test barns with the traditional, dark, quiet, and totally enclosed stalls for the horses to be tested. To my gelding, those were totally unacceptable. Nick explained very graphically to the racing world why he did not like being placed in any "dark hole of Calcutta" by obliterating a test stall at each facility.

A Thoroughbred trainer who witnessed the kicking destruction told me that in the future I could insist the testing be done back in Nick's own stall. For his wins thereafter, that is how it was done. Nick reveled in this new ceremony. He now had an opportunity to show his neighbors and stable mates that he had accomplished something wonderful that particular day. He was very important, obviously verified by the entourage of racing commission staff trailing behind him as we made our way back to his stall after each race he won.

I had to learn how to gallop my own horses, because when Arabians first started racing, the better gallop riders at the tracks would not ride them, claiming there was "too much neck" in their faces. That was not a problem for me, because I already rode English, broke and trained my own horses, and weighed 112 pounds. But I was 5 feet, 8 inches tall, and so I always felt like a grasshopper folded up on that tiny saddle on the back of a galloping horse. Baryshnikov galloped like a true race horse, even with his idiosyncrasies. Consequently, he taught me how to ride properly in an exercise saddle, although I probably never felt totally secure.

The Arabians could only have stalls at the bigger tracks on race days, so we would haul in to exercise our horses. In fact, Arabians were housed in goat stalls the first years they ran at one of the fairground's tracks in Washington. True story. When I hauled in to Les Bois Park at Boise, I would tie my horses to the side of the horse trailer. Can you imagine a Cigar or a Funny Cide tied to the side of a horse trailer, awaiting his turn to gallop? Not in a million years! Mine were well-behaved, because we went out to the foothills for exercise in between track visits and they were accustomed to being tied to the trailer. The horse trailer was their home away from home.

One particular Saturday I had taken Nick out to Les Bois Park for a gallop. We were in our second lap on the far turn about five lanes out from the rail when two Thoroughbreds came by on the inside breezing. Many Arabians become bored easily, and Nick was one of them. He wanted to work briskly, not gallop boring laps, and so he was looking for an excuse, any excuse, to relieve his boredom. He immediately jumped about three lanes out to the right, never breaking stride.

Initially, I was able to stay right with him, but by now we were perilously close to the outside rail, where all the Saturday morning railbirds were perched. These are the owners who come out on the weekends to watch their horses being galloped. Nick took note of these railbirds: *Oh my God, something new!* He jumped back about three lanes toward the middle of the track. That was the end for me, and off I went!

At first, I thought I had been knocked cuckoo, because I couldn't focus on anything. Some of the railbirds helped me off the track, while another picked up the lens that had popped out of my glasses frame. Once I had the complete pair of glasses, everything came back into focus just fine, and I began to look for my horse. Somebody said, "He went that way!"—meaning, he had left the track via the starting gate chute.

Another trainer, who had witnessed the episode, was on a golf cart and offered to take me to find my horse. Still somewhat shaken, I readily accepted the offer of transportation and assistance.

Looking off the track, I could see my truck and trailer parked in the little grassy area between the shed rows and the race track. I hoped Nick had headed for that patch of grass, but he was nowhere to be seen. We rode in that golf cart up and down every shed row, to no avail; my horse had vanished. Finally, we went to the main gate to warn them that there was a horse missing or loose. My trainer friend with the golf cart thought I should call the sheriff. I agreed.

My stomach had that sinking feeling, like when you know something is going to end badly. I had just seen a heartbreaking Barbara Walters special on the charro rodeos (now, fortunately, outlawed) in California, where the lives of many horses, including stolen or unwanted racehorses, often ended in tragic circumstances.

We headed back to the race office to use the phone. The word had gotten around the backside that my good horse was missing, and several trainers joined us to offer words of encouragement.

One man said, "Your other horse has been standing in your trailer quite awhile. Would you like me to go take care of it while you wait for the sheriff?"

I looked at him blankly. What "other" horse? I had brought only one horse to the track that day. The man explained that he had just walked past the side of my trailer on his way up to the race office and could see a horse standing inside. Well, guess who?

Baryshnikov, apparently knowing he was in deep doo-doo for dumping me on the track and running off, had nosed the unlatched trailer door open and climbed back in. There stood my missing horse, helping himself to a full hay bag, as he had been for well over an hour. He looked at me dismissively as if to say, "Ho hum. You were worried about me?"

I, of course, threw my arms around his sleek neck, crying, and told him how glad I was to see him safe, once again reinforcing his questionable behavior.

Pam Karlsgodt Roylance

This story first appeared under the title "A Tale from the Track" in the Idaho Arabian Breeders Association *newsletter, August 2004.*

Crossing Over

It was a perfect day for a horseback ride. The air was warm for late October, and the sumac blazed crimson amid yellow foliage in the autumn sun. Trigger was at the far side of the pasture, so I whistled for him.

The gelding lifted his head, turned, and faced my direction, twitching his ears. Trigger wasn't a registered American Paint, but that didn't matter to me. The way he stood in the pasture, his black, white, and brown coat shining in the sunlight, made me think he was the most beautiful animal in the world. He was just the right height—tall enough for my dad to use for herding cattle and short enough for me, a five-foot-two teenager, to ride.

I whistled again, but the horse didn't move. I filled my pockets with cracked corn and dragged the saddlery across the field, the bridle flopping against my shoulder. Trigger turned and faced my direction, head high and ears erect. As I walked toward him, I twisted my ankle and fell, then got up and limped in his direction.

I fell a lot because I had polio when I was little. Though I couldn't run or jump, I could walk up to a mile if I didn't hurry. I learned to climb on a horse by standing on one leg and pulling myself up. My father had taught me to be proud of what I could do.

I caught the disease in 1942, when we lived in Detroit and a polio epidemic struck. After a year of therapy, the partial paralysis in my back and legs improved enough for me to walk. However, the doctors were not impressed. They said I was "trick walking," because I couldn't use the proper muscles. In 1948, we moved to the Midwest to live on the family farm. My parents wanted to escape the creeping urban sprawl of the big city.

I missed the city sidewalks. They were easier to walk on than the farm's rocky ground. Uneven surfaces caused me to fall and skin my knees. I missed going places in the city alone or with buddies. It was lonely living in the country, and I missed my city friends. My folks worried because of my quick temper.

When I was thirteen years old, Daddy told neighbors that I had to learn self-control. He meant I got mad too easily. "She has to learn to allow for other people's limitations," he would say.

His solution was to buy me a blind horse, Trigger. Dad insisted that I could be Trigger's eyes and he could be my feet.

My father taught me how to handle the horse in our fenced-in barn lot. Learning how to handle him was easy, but then my father had me dismount and put Trigger in the stall. While the horse was confined, I practiced bridling and saddling him, which went well enough. Mounting him by myself was more difficult. Most people mount their horses on the left side. I couldn't put my weak left foot in the stirrup and use that leg to swing myself into the saddle. Fortunately, Trigger had been trained to be mounted from either side, so I was able to get on from the right.

As long as my Paint was in the stall, he couldn't step away when I climbed on. Though horses are trained not to sidestep, Dad worried about how Trigger might react when I mounted him out in the pasture. But I was sure I could handle, mount, and ride him anywhere.

On that crisp October day, I wanted to climb on my horse's back and go for a ride. Trigger obviously had something else in mind, because as I approached him, he turned and walked away. I dropped the saddle, sighed, and followed him to where the fences crossed. After I cornered him, I grabbed the rope halter and pulled the bridle over his ears.

"Here, have some grain," I said, thrusting some under his nose. When he opened his mouth, I slipped the bit between his teeth.

"Good boy!" I cooed.

After positioning the bridle and buckling the straps, I took the reins in hand and led him up the fence to the saddle. "I know I can saddle you, Trigger, but can I mount you out here?" I had never done that. But I decided that if I was going to ride, I had to learn how to get on his back no matter where we were.

"Don't let your horse side away from you as you mount," I remembered my father saying. "Keep his left side against a barrier."

With Trigger's side against the fence, I put the blanket on his back and positioned the saddle. I reached under his belly, grabbed the strap, pulled it around, and cinched it. Then I wrapped the reins around the saddle horn and thrust my right foot into the stirrup. I grabbed his mane and used the saddle horn to pull myself up. But the saddle slid around his belly with me clinging to it upside down. Plop! I landed on my backside in fresh manure. Trigger backed around me with his head pulled down to my face. I still held the reins.

"You stupid beast!" I yelled. Trigger laid back his sensitive ears.

My foot came out of the stirrup as I kicked and pounded the ground. I slapped at Trigger, missed and hit the saddle horn. My hand stung. He jerked his head back.

"Oh, Trigger, I'm sorry." I reached up and wrapped my arms around his neck and cried.

I stood up and unfastened the saddle, repositioned it, and pulled the cinch taut. Once I was secure in the saddle, I gripped the reins tight. The horse pranced a few steps, settled down, and cantered out of the field to the creek-gravel road.

Trigger slowed to a walk when his feet hit the rocky road and picked his way over the stones. The road's surface was creek gravel, a mixture of rocks and mud common to waterways of the area. It was passable in most weather, but truck wheels had cut ruts in it. I had difficulty walking on uneven ground and my horse could not see the road's surface, so I understood his need for level footing. I guided him to the smoothest side of the road. When a truck came into view, I brought Trigger to a halt on the shoulder of the road.

"Drivers may honk their horns and frighten your horse," Dad had cautioned before we set out. "Be safe; make him stand on the side of the road until they pass."

Trigger was well trained in this practice—too well. After the truck was gone, an airplane flew overhead. At the sound of the plane's motor, Trigger stepped to the roadside and stood motionless. I kicked my heels and flopped the reins.

"Oh, come on, Trigger! That airplane won't hurt you. Let's go!" I yelled and pulled on the reins.

In response, he reared, came down, and reared again. Shaken, I waited until the engine noise faded. I decided that because Trigger was unable to guide himself in a sightless world, he could pause at the sound of an airplane motor. After the plane was gone, we rode on.

Cows in the field raised their heads and horses whinnied as we trotted the roads. Hay stacks and corn shocks dotted the fields. My mount and I were in great spirits.

When we came to where a split-log bridge crossed a stream, Trigger slowed to a walk. He stopped when his foot touched the plank. I urged him onward. He shied, stepped sideways, and almost fell into the water.

"Whoa, Trigger, back." I pulled on the reins. "What's wrong, boy?"

He continued to step backward until we were safe on the road again.

I studied the bridge. There was nothing wrong with it. I tried to guide him forward, but Trigger balked and shied.

"What's the matter?" I kicked his side.

He reared. I slapped his flanks as he raised again. Then he danced, down on all fours and up again, until I slipped off his backside. I hit the ground, rolled out of the range of his kicking feet, and lay there, bawling in frustration and imagined pain.

I sat up, wiped my eyes on my sleeve, and realized neither of us was hurt. Trigger stood at the roadside. I got up and walked over and petted him while I considered my plight. *Now, what will I do? A horse has to cross bridges. I am not about to stop coming this way just because he doesn't like the sound of his own footsteps.*

I drank water from my canteen while Trigger munched the grass.

"It's your job to train that horse. You've got to teach him what you want the minute you spot a problem," Daddy had said. "You can't wait until later—not if you want him to understand."

My father would have expected me to teach Trigger to cross the bridge and to do it without delay.

After I poured water into my cupped hand and offered it to Trigger, I took the reins and led him to the center of the road.

"Okay, Trigger, here we go," I said, tugging on the reins as I walked ahead. "One step . . . that's right. Now another. See? That's not so bad. Take your time. Now your hind foot. A little further. Good!" The hollow sounds of the boards grew less ominous as we crossed and our feet touched solid ground on the other side. We crossed the bridge again, back and forth, until Trigger no longer resisted my lead.

I led him through a ditch and into a field and positioned him against a fence so I could mount. Then I guided him back to the road, speaking in a soft voice and patting his neck. My horse walked toward the edge of the bridge, taking slow, even steps. I let him choose his path to cross to the other side. When his feet touched solid ground, I laid the right rein against his neck and pulled on the left, guiding him in a semicircle, praising him softly as he made the turn. Then we crossed back to where we'd started. It was time to head home.

I tugged on the left rein again until Trigger turned and faced the bridge. Then I flipped both reins and shouted, "Let's go!" This time, he crossed the bridge with quick, confident steps. And I'd crossed a bridge of sorts, too—between the island of doubt and the land of possibility.

Trigger and I trotted all the way home. We were in sync again—each trusting the other to do all that we were able.

Ina Mae Brooks

A version of this story was first published under the title "Lessons from a Four-Foot Tutor" in the e-zine Breath and Shadow, *Fall 2006.*

Too Precious to Waste

Avery is my Fjord-Paint gelding. I think he's a Fjord. I know he's a Paint; that part is hard to miss. If his former owner is to be believed, he is the product of no fewer than three distinct breeds—Fjord, Paint, Percheron—and quarter horse. He looks like such an amalgamation of all four that you really can't see any of them—except the Paint, which is, again, hard to miss.

Avery came to me at his mother's side when he was only a week old. About the spring of his sixth year, I suddenly realized he was fast becoming a permanent pasture ornament. It's not that I didn't like him. Avery was a wonderful fellow—smart and cute, and to his eternal credit, he liked me (yep, it was the treats) and liked to work. He'd been ground-driven, lunged, and worked in hand until we were both sick of it and ready for something new. I backed him, finally, in the fall of his fourth year. And then I stalled or stopped cold, whichever perspective you choose.

I was in my forties, and since I'd lost my gentle, old, true-blue mare a few years back, I hadn't ridden regularly. The thought of working a greenie made my bones ache, and the longer I delayed, the older I became, and the older I got, the more my (theoretically) old bones ached at the thought of getting on, riding, and working a young green horse.

Okay, who was I kidding? It wasn't "getting on" I was afraid of. It was getting off. I'm not talking about the nice, controlled getting off: stop, dismount, pat horse, walk away safely. The "getting off" I dreaded, and envisioned, involved lying in the dirt thinking nasty words that would upset my mother. This "getting off" involved a *thud!*—followed by a mental inventory of bruises, bumps, possible broken bones, and just how many sick days I actually have left at work.

Speaking of which, I work nights and usually get home about six o'clock in the morning, an early enough hour that I could (okay, should) take advantage of the quiet mornings to work Avery. But I was stuck in the same old rut: come home, kick off my shoes, slip into comfy clothes, sit in front of the TV or computer until it seduced me into sleepiness, climb into my cozy bed. And zip! Another day has gone by in which Avery's most productive activity has been to mow and fertilize the field, which is more than I can say for myself.

Then one morning, I don't know why, I decided to do something . . . different. The day certainly started out the same: I got off work and headed home with thoughts of chilling out on the sofa for a few hours before shuffling off to dreamland floating through my head. But the idea came to me from somewhere—probably fueled by that large café mocha—that I would get on Avery and, with all due respect to the advertising genies, "Just do it!"

Then, once home, I thought, *Gee the car needs to be cleaned out.*

Cleaned out the car.

Then I thought, *Gee, I should check my e-mail.*

Checked my e-mail.

Then I thought, *Gee, I haven't read that magazine.*

Picked up that magazine, sat in front of an open window, and . . . looked out.

It was a late spring morning in northern Virginia, and it was a rarity, a gem, a real beauty. The sort you don't want to waste sitting in the house reading a six-month-old magazine. The sort that turns the sky a liquid blue. The sort where the sunlight turns every leaf and blade of grass into emeralds and tourmalines and peridots, and they don't merely shine with the light, they glow. There would be few more of those cool, breezy June mornings, because July and summer and air conditioners and humidity and bugs were just around the corner.

I sat there infuriated with myself. Hating myself for wasting that morning, for wasting Avery, for taking counsel of my fears.

Fifteen minutes later, I had changed, gathered saddle and bridle, and was walking toward Avery with halter in hand. Now, here is where literary license takes a hard right toward harsh reality. Avery, who in all his years has never failed to come up to me, took one look at the halter and hightailed it for the hills.

Harsh lesson number one: Your horse is not a romantic, idealistic creature. Your goals are not always his goals. If he lives his life as a pasture ornament, he may not share in your regrets. He may hold fast to his contention that wonderful June mornings are for bug-free grazing, not for fulfilling silly human expectations.

Lesson number two: There is a lot more caffeine in a large mocha than I had previously thought.

Lesson number three: Avery really is a nice guy.

He let me chase him for a bit, then finally stopped and came back, pleased at the joke he had played on me. He was antsy while I groomed and tacked him up, but he seemed happy for the attention.

Eventually, I got on. I have to admit, there were a few stops and starts, and I kept thinking how hard the ground looked and how sassy Avery was behaving, but then, finally, I just climbed on.

Avery took it all in stride, confident his crazy owner had some grand plan and that in the end there would be treats, lots of treats. I didn't disappoint him, but then, he didn't disappoint me.

That left me with this resolution: I didn't want to be wasteful anymore.

Now, I'm not talking about the "wasteful" that involves less toilet flushing or more trips to recycling bins or conserving hay. I mean the kind of wasteful that squanders joy and friendship and love. The kind of wasteful that kept me in the house on a beautiful day and kept me from developing the partnership I knew I could have with Avery.

I wasn't asking for much: a ride through the woods, a canter in the field, a friend to share a hidden trail with, to occasionally fall off of and, hopefully, to climb back on. Neither of us was getting any younger, and if I didn't start now, would I ever? In the grand scheme of the world, it's really such a small thing to want, but in the small scheme of my world, it means something more. Like small pebbles in small ponds, the ripples always travel outward, so this one seemingly small good thing—working with my horse—would lead to another and another small good thing.

So here's to café mochas. And here's to more mornings too precious to waste—no matter what the weather's like, no matter what's on TV, no matter what needs to be done, no matter what the ground looks like from the saddle—no matter what. Go out and ride! It's a beautiful day.

Christine K. Thomas

The Rescue Boat

Outside the small town of Coburg, along the banks of Oregon's McKenzie River, a rescue boat disrupts the quiet of this warm spring day. I wonder if this is a practice run or if a real rescue is in progress. The boat moves further up the river until I can no longer see or hear it. I sit down on a rock to rest my hiking legs. On the other side, a group of horses graze on verdant fields. A sorrel colt looks over at me. My heart gallops inside my chest like it did forty years ago when I first laid eyes on my filly.

She had just come off the Nevada range with other wild horses, and though I didn't know it then, she was my rescue boat.

When I first saw her, she looked at me as if to say, "Who are you?"

I straddled my long legs over the corral and stared back at her. I wanted to shout, "I'm the luckiest ten-year-old in the world. I've always wanted a horse, and now my dream is coming true!"

My stepsister, Patty, and her husband owned a large Nevada ranch. Dad and I had driven all night from Idaho to get there. Patty was anxious to see Dad again. He'd just returned from a tour of duty for the air force. But I was the happiest, because Patty had talked Dad into letting me have any of the wild horses I wanted.

Patty nudged me. "You've got your eye on that filly. Are you sure that's the one?"

"She's perfect."

"You won't be able to ride her for almost two years."

"That's okay," I said and climbed down from the fence. "We'll be the best of friends by then."

I tucked some of my blond hair behind my ears and looked up at Patty. Twelve years older than I was, she was the prettiest lady I'd ever known. She was a ranch woman, outside all day long, her cheeks naturally rosy from fresh air.

"The foal will need to be bottle-fed," Patty said.

"I already know all about that. I babysat for the first time this year. I fed Mrs. Loomis's baby lots of bottles."

Patty laughed. "Well, babies and colts are a little different. But I think you can handle her."

She waved to Jake, one of her hired hands. "Round up that filly for my sister."

Jake made a lasso with his rope and then swung it above his head like the cowboys on TV. He jumped down into the corral, and the horses scattered, even the little foal. But soon he lassoed her and scooped her up like a sack of flour. Her legs flailed as he put her in the holding pen. She whinnied a forlorn sound.

I rushed over to her side. "It's okay, little girl. I'll be right back with a bottle."

She stared at me with her big brown eyes, and I knew she believed me. I didn't want to walk away. I was afraid that this would all turn out to be a dream, like it had been a million times before.

Patty motioned me toward the barn. This was for real.

Inside, Patty handed me the largest bottle I'd ever seen. "Put in a scoop full," she said and pointed toward a large bag of horse formula on the floor that leaned against the side of an old sink.

As I put the yellow powder into the bottle, some of it fell onto my hand. It felt like flour but smelled sweet like whipped cream on strawberries.

Patty turned on the faucet, and cold water gushed out. "You want the water to be warm, like the bottles you made for the Loomis baby," she said.

I tested it with my wrist. When it was just right, I filled the bottle. Patty and I took turns stirring until all the lumps disappeared.

"Hand me a top from the drawer," she said.

I reached in and felt rubber nipples the size of cow udders.

"Whoa! Where do you get all this big stuff?"

She smiled. "At a feed store. You have one in your town, but I'll send you home with enough supplies to last a few weeks."

She grabbed a halter and lead rope off the wall, and we walked back outside.

I giggled as my filly greedily slurped down the bottle. I had to hold tight; she tugged so hard. "You poor little girl. I don't think you've eaten in days."

"What do you think happened to her mom?" I asked Patty.

"Probably a cougar. Given another day, it would have gotten her too."

I stroked the foal's face. She pulled away for a second, then quickly returned to the bottle. "Don't worry, little lady. I'll take good care of you."

Over the next few years, I did. And Lady and I did become the best of friends. Even though she was the orphan, I needed her more. I began to tell her all the secrets I'd been holding deep inside. Like a locket opened, I revealed everything.

One day I told Lady my biggest secret. She'd just finished eating, and I'd filled her water trough and cleaned the manure out of her stall. We lay together in the fresh hay. I rested my head upon her soft belly that rose and lifted to the beat of my own heart. I let out a big sigh.

I told her how three years ago, when Dad was away, bad stuff had happened to my little sister, Sally, and me. I had tried to tell my mom, but it hadn't worked out the way I'd hoped. Mom sat at the table, reading her *Good Housekeeping* magazine. Sally and I had just finished our lunch of tomato soup, grilled cheese sandwiches, and chocolate milk. Sally went to play as I cleared off my dishes.

I almost didn't tell Mom; I was so scared. But finally I said, "Brad's been hurting me and Sally."

Mom looked up from her magazine. "What do you mean?"

"He makes us touch him. He kisses us and makes us do other stuff. Yucky things I don't like."

She looked at me.

I waited. I wanted a hug. Something.

"Well, we can't tell your father," she finally said. "Brad's his best friend. Your father asked him to keep an eye on us while he's away. Brad's been good to us. You don't want to break your father's heart, do you?"

She returned to her *Good Housekeeping.*

My courage melted away like spring snow on the Nevada plains. I nearly choked on words I wanted to say but now couldn't—words like, "What about my heart, Mommy?"

I spent the next two years doing the best I could to protect my sister and me from him. Sometimes I succeeded, sometimes I didn't.

One day after school when Mom was away at work, I was sitting on the front porch. I saw him coming down the street in his blue truck. I ran inside and locked all the doors. I closed the curtains. He pounded on the front door. I became more scared as the sounds got louder and louder. *What if he found a way inside?* I grabbed my sister, and together we ran into the bathroom. I locked the door and pulled every towel out of the top cabinet, then pushed her inside. I covered her with the towels and closed the cabinet doors.

She started to cry.

"Quiet," I snapped. "He'll hear us."

The pounding continued. I heard the clicking of his shoes as he walked around the back of the house. I scooped out the towels from the bottom cabinet and wiggled inside. I covered myself as best I could.

But I was worried that even though he couldn't see me, my pounding heart would give us away. We huddled inside the separate cupboards until I heard the screech of his angry tires. I felt bad that I'd made a grown-up angry, but I was also happy. I'd won.

I buried my face into Lady's mane. "Mom told me I couldn't tell Dad, Lady. I've always been too embarrassed to tell anyone else, but I felt I could tell you."

Salty tears streamed down my cheeks. She whinnied softly. I looked up at her, and she nuzzled my face. She understood.

That summer when Dad returned home from Thailand and Patty sent me home with Lady, no one realized what I'd been given. Lady saved my life. For several years, she was the only living thing I could really talk to. She listened to my every word and kept me from drowning, from going under when life had become too much for me to bear. Lady was someone I could trust, and eventually, in time, she helped me to heal enough so that I could trust in others.

A few years passed before I told another friend, a human that time. In those days, most kids kept such things to themselves. When it became more acceptable to confront molesters, I discovered that he had died a few years before, alone in a hotel room, with a bottle of alcohol in his hands. Lady was gone by then, too, but still, when I learned of his demise I felt her by my side, nudging my shoulder, telling me it was okay. It was time to move on.

Long before it was popular in our culture to see the horse as a healing instrument, I, as a young girl of ten, discovered this for myself. Although, at the time, I didn't understand the benefits that would be derived from telling Lady my story, it didn't matter. What mattered was she was there when my mother couldn't be. What mattered was she listened. That little colt was my rescue boat.

Deanna Stollar

Of Cowboys and Courage

I was eight years old in the spring of 1945. My parents had just gone through a divorce, and my Uncle Jimmy had been killed shortly before V-E Day.

Uncle Jimmy was a cowboy. During rodeo season, he'd sent me pictures of him on various broncos, waving his cowboy hat while the horse tried to buck him off. I guess you could say he had been my hero. Before he went to war, we visited him and my Aunt Jean on their ranch in Washington state, and there were photos of me riding his roan mare while he led the horse. Try as I might, though, I couldn't remember it.

That summer of 1945, Mom worked as a trumpet player entertaining in USOs and clubs throughout the San Francisco Bay Area. Aunt Jean suggested that, due to Mom's irregular hours, it might be good for me to spend the summer with her; plus, she'd have some company and help around the place. So Mom and I boarded the train and headed north. Mom would return to San Francisco the following day because of her work.

We arrived late, and Aunt Jean led me to my room. Soon, I was dreaming of being a cowboy just like my Uncle Jimmy. He had been a *real* cowboy, not like the ones we kids saw in the movies.

After Mom left the next morning, Aunt Jean reacquainted me with the vaguely familiar setting. There was no indoor plumbing, but the privy was just a short way from the house. For water, a well with a hand pump was just outside the kitchen door. An old cowboy hat hung on a peg by the door, and as I reached for it, Aunt Jean grabbed my hand.

"It was your Uncle Jimmy's. He hung it there the day he left. I don't let anyone touch it," she said and then smiled apologetically.

I quickly withdrew my hand.

Outside were chickens, a couple of cows, and a pen containing several pigs. What little money Aunt Jean had was from Uncle Jimmy's death benefit and from whatever income she got from the livestock, milk, and occasional boarding of a horse or two.

During my stay I was expected to help with the chores, which included feeding the animals. I couldn't believe how nasty the pigs smelled. The heck with the pigs! I wanted to see the horses. Aunt Jean explained that she had to sell off all but one of the horses due to financial problems. The only one left was Roany, Uncle Jimmy's roan mare, the horse he'd let me ride when I was small.

A year before, a terrible fire had partially destroyed the barn. Roany had been inside. The mare had managed to escape, but not before she'd suffered the loss of an eye from a firebrand that dropped from the rafters. A new but smaller barn had been built by contributing neighbors who'd held Uncle Jimmy in high esteem. However, Roany had refused to go inside, so Aunt Jean had built a lean-to structure onto one side of the building. It was open on three sides. Roany would stand in the middle of it, her front legs splayed wide, and when she saw us approach, she'd toss her head and then back slowly away.

Aunt Jean took hold of my shoulder and turned me around. "Gary, you won't be able to ride her. Since the fire, no one has been able to ride her, not even me. I brought you here because you needed to see for yourself and understand."

A short but horrible scar ran across the mare's permanently closed right eye. As we slowly approached, she reared up and lifted her head high, showing the white of her one good eye, shiny and bright and full of fear. Then she backed away.

Aunt Jean gave me a carrot and, with my heart tripping in my chest, I held it out to the animal. Instead of taking it, she backed away even farther, tossing her head and pawing the ground.

My aunt sighed. "Just leave it there on the ground. She'll eat it when we leave."

Dejected, I chucked the carrot and stuffed my hands in my pockets. As we walked away, Aunt Jean told me she didn't want me near the horse without her.

"I just don't trust her anymore, Gary. You might get hurt."

That was okay. I didn't care anymore about horses or about being a cowboy like Uncle Jimmy. I just wanted to go home. I missed my folks. I hadn't been thinking about "chores" when I said I would spend the summer here. And I hated pigs!

Later, in bed that night, I felt a bit selfish. I thought about Aunt Jean running the whole place by herself and about how I'd been thinking only about me and wanting to ride horses and be a cowboy. I hadn't considered the fact that my mother's sister was barely making it and was still grieving the loss of her husband. But I was a boy, and my newfound compassion didn't stop me from thinking about my own interests.

When my morning chores were done, I'd secretly go out to the barn and see Roany. After many mornings of bringing out handfuls of carrots, I was able to get Roany to follow me around the pasture by holding out a carrot and then dropping it on the ground closer and closer to my feet. I'd been at the ranch for about a month when, finally, one day she took the carrot from my hand. I was elated. Each day we repeated the routine until I was able to rub my hand above her nose and even brush her out. I felt that horrible scar, rough and tight, so unlike the smoothness of the rest of her. It was so sad, and I started to cry.

Roany stood there for a long time, trembling, and then she stepped forward and nuzzled my shoulder. I remember thinking that maybe she sensed I was missing Mom and Dad the same way she was missing Uncle Jimmy. Through some sort of foolish exuberance, I reached around her neck and pulled myself onto her back. For a moment, she just stood there trembling—and then she promptly bucked me off. I landed on the ground, the wind knocked out of me.

We repeated this routine for a couple of weeks. Each time I tried to mount her, she'd buck me off. Looking back, it was probably more like a shrug for her than an actual buck, for I was small for my age and couldn't really ride.

It was in the second or maybe the third week of this that Roany stood over me and nickered softly. I got up, reached into my pocket, and held out another carrot to her. "Please, Roany," I whispered.

She moved forward and took the carrot, all the while watching me with her one good eye. I stroked her muzzle, reached up and petted her neck, wrapped her mane around my hand, and hoisted myself onto her back. This time she stood still, and I could feel her tremble. I stroked her neck, leaned over and pet-ted her cheek, then gave her another carrot, all the time talking softly to her.

"C'mon, girl. Let's show Aunt Jean what we can do."

Still trembling, she haltingly moved forward. Her walk became faster and then broke into a trot, and I had to hang onto her mane for dear life while my butt bounced on her back. I was terrified, but from somewhere in the back of my head I could almost hear Uncle Jimmy telling me to hug her tightly with my knees, and so I did, while keeping a death grip on her mane.

"Aunt Jean," I yelled toward the house. "Look, Aunt Jean!"

Roany had turned so our backs were to the house, but when we turned again, there was my aunt on the porch, her hand covering her mouth. Roany stopped short, nearly throwing me off, as Aunt Jean ran to us.

"I can't believe it! Oh, my God," she cried out. Her eyes were brimming with tears.

I slid off Roany's back, and we went into the barn. My aunt showed me Roany's tack and how to put it on.

It didn't happen overnight, but as that wonderful animal slowly gained back her trust, I learned to ride her, first with just the halter and rope, then with the bit and bridle, and finally with Uncle Jimmy's old saddle, even though the stirrups had to be shortened as far up as they could go.

For my birthday present that year, Aunt Jean gave me Uncle Jimmy's old cowboy hat. Of course, it didn't fit, and we had to fold newspaper into the sweatband, but it was the best birthday present I'd ever received, other than my horse, Roany, of course.

Gary B. Luerding

At Clyde's Pace

I was living back in Maryland, working on a 150-acre horse farm. It was just me and the horse trainer, Bob, long and wiry and unhappy, who never talked, and when he did talk you wished he wouldn't. I would brush the horses, clean the barn, clean the pool, clean the house, working outside, breathing real air, taking in all that land, miles of trails in the woods, the dewy wet tiles of the Amish-built barn, the carriages under tarps in the barn breeze-way. I would walk down paths and pick up frogs. The owner was never there; he was Austrian, always traveling around. He had started as a Mercedes mechanic and then started his own security company and now focused on being rich.

One day I had brushed the white Lipizzan, Jaggy, and held him while Bob put on the harness, the masses of leather that didn't make any sense, the shiny silver loops. When everything was laced and tight and connected, Bob drew the wooden cart up and through the loops, and we attached Jaggy with the straps. Then Bob climbed in and gathered the whip and reins and gestured that I move out of the way. The horse burst forth, clattering from the barn to where I waited in my dirty clothes. Bob stopped the cart and said the only words he'd ever said that mattered to me, "Get on." I jumped onto the seat, and we were driving.

Twenty years I'd been on horses' backs, now here I was behind one, on wheels, and it was terrifying. You're too far from the mouth. The control is shaky. There aren't any shocks; you feel every bump on the dirt road. The carriage is precarious. The horse is bright and alert—maybe too alert.

Then we were in the woods, on winding paths, and fear lurked everywhere: a bird flies up, a blind corner, a steep incline. Then we were out on the road, with pastureland on either side and neighbors in tractors, and Jaggy didn't seem to mind. And suddenly I was in the 1800s, full-skirted, fair, hatted, in the sunshine.

We got back to the farm, and I got off and started unhooking everything, trying to remember how everything unhooked. The horse was sweating, and my heart was dancing. I belonged forever in this past. This horse and cart were simple. They made sense.

It was just a physical manifestation of what I'd been doing in my head for years: bringing on the past. I never let anything go. Ex-boyfriends, old houses, long-ago pets, my parents' marriage crumbling—it was all there, fresh, on the top. My memories were more real than my now, and now I had a vehicle, drawn by a horse, that I could carry it all in, and I'd never have to leave anything behind. In fact, I could *stay* behind, that was the point. No mechanical engine; this engine was alive, required love and brushing and training and care, required soft talking to and human touch. It felt. You could feel its pulse. I could hold it all. *Jump in my wagon, I can hold you too.*

Five years later, I was living outside of Los Angeles in a horse community called Shadow Hills. My husband was working, and I had two babies under four. I had never stopped thinking of driving; its mystery had seeped its way into my blood. I picked up the free *Horsetrader* magazine at the feed store and saw an ad for a wedding-carriage business for sale, with a carriage, a white horse, a Web site, harnesses, everything. I wanted to go back in time, and here was a place I could do that, every day.

My husband, Barry, said buying a horse-drawn carriage business was a sure way to lose money. We had just bought a house we couldn't afford. We couldn't take out a loan to buy a business that wouldn't make enough money to live on.

I was obsessed. I e-mailed the woman who was selling the business constantly, as if I were going to buy it. I made Barry go up to look at the farm and see the equipment. The huge truck. The winch that pulls the carriage up and down out of the trailer. The winch is what sealed it for me. *There is no way I could do this!* I immediately thought. I couldn't operate that. I barely knew how to drive a horse; I'd only practiced once or twice. The trailer itself was forty feet long.

Driving away after seeing all the equipment, I told my husband, "Okay, you're right, it's too hard."

But he said, "I see why you like it. The carriages are beautiful."

I was bummed, thinking I wasn't getting the business. Then I was walking down the road near my house with the kids in strollers and bikes, and my neighbor stopped her car to talk to me. I told her I was dying to drive horses, that I had found this business but couldn't afford to buy it.

Two days later, she said she wanted to add to her horse rental business. I could work for her.

Barry and I again went up the winding roads to show her where Clyde was living, the giant white ghost horse that would be my carriage traveling companion. Winding canyons and uninhabited mountains, with wire fencing and horses dotting the pastures occasionally, all seem surreal in Los Angeles, like you're cheating on the city by being out in the country this close in.

It was dark, and there was the farm. We saw the carriages in their carriage house, under covers, and we went past rows of pastured horses, and then we came upon the biggest, whitest horse I'd ever seen. I thought I had seen a lot of horses. But none compared with Clyde, a Percheron, almost 18 hands high, with his big white head, his lips bigger than my whole face, his hair hung in his eyes like a surfer who'd dropped out of school. In the dusk, he was like the full moon, glimmering with a shadow on the ground.

The current owner told me his feet were terrible, and my heart sunk, like buying a truck with four flat tires. But he was a magical horse, a floating carousel all on his own.

I helped my neighbor buy all the equipment. I made several trips up with her hired men to load it all, the stacks of leather, boxes of horse shoes, carriage, and training cart.

Then, months later, with no practice, she had me do her first booking, a wedding proposal in Pasadena. We trailered Clyde to Pasadena. As we got him harnessed up, old people smiled at his big old head and the carriage. They were in the crosswalk or on the sidewalk, bent over, and they looked up as they passed, contentment on their faces, remembering. *Look, the ice man is here.*

I drove Clyde around the block, a trial run, because I really had no idea how to drive. It was dusk. We turned the corner and we were trotting, and it was lyrical. Then we were passing a school, and about a hundred school kids at camp in the playground yelled "horse!" and started screaming and charging at us en masse. I cringed, hoping Clyde wouldn't bolt, that I wouldn't die there. Clyde flicked an ear at them. Then it felt like slow motion, the kids running alongside us, the carriage decorated with white silk flowers and white gauze, like a French movie.

At the designated spot, I picked up the groom-to-be, Gene, a well-dressed Taiwanese guy who was going to propose to his unknowing girlfriend, Jenny. She was having dinner with friends at a restaurant around the corner.

"I just flew in from Shanghai to surprise her," he said as he got in the carriage.

My heart skipped. *God, I hope she says yes.* "How long have you been dating?" I asked.

"Nine months. Sort of quick. But when you know, it's . . ." He shrugged.

I hoped he knew.

His cell phone rang. He'd gotten the go-ahead.

We started off around the block.

I realized that on this job I'd get to intimately witness pivotal points in people's lives. We'd turn the corner and this guy would either get engaged or be tragically rebuffed in front of all his friends and me and Clyde.

We got to the busy corner where the restaurant was, and a bunch of people were standing in the courtyard behind the fence. Suddenly, everyone was looking toward us and talking excitedly. Gene looked at me, clutching the flowers. "Should I get up?" he asked.

I stared at the people. "I don't know."

He got up, and a young, attractive woman, obviously Jenny, came from between people, saw the carriage and Gene, and her hand went to her mouth and her face squeezed up and she started to cry. It was so beautiful I almost cried too. Gene leapt down to her. She was paralyzed as her friends laughed and as he swept in and handed her the flowers and hugged her, and she was still crying and he was on his knees.

I'm guessing Jenny said yes; she had to say yes.

I took them on a ride, dropped them off, then I began the best part of my drive. Dusk had turned to darkness. The streets were lined with overhanging trees, and the houses we passed loomed large, two stories, like estates, and it felt like I could come to call and a stable attendant would rush out to hold the horse while I went in to meet the land owner.

People in cars slowed down as they passed, smiling, waving, taking pictures, stopping their lives momentarily. The best part was their faces, their momentary unexpected pause, the wondrous look of nostalgia at our carriage on their regular city streets, in their regular busy lives.

They continued on, moving ahead at their fast pace, hurrying off to somewhere, and I just let Clyde walk, listening to his feet echoing off the pavement, clucking to him until I finally felt like I was going the right speed. I was steering him with the lines across his white back, and he was listening, flicking his ears back, confident that our ride would be interesting, keeping us at an even pace. Everything felt simple and relaxed.

The night had nearly blacked out the sky, the moon was almost full, and the carriage was empty, so I could take all the time I wanted and count the seconds of my life going by, just enjoy being out for a walk with Clyde, the breeze lifting his mane, in my long black skirt with white petticoat, back in time.

On a side street corner, as we ambled past, an old lady smiled at us. *Fresh milk delivery.*

Driving home on the grim, gray freeway afterward, I thought about how much effort it was to harness and unharness the heavy leather, to load up Clyde, the carriage, the trailer. It was time-consuming, laborious, and physically tiring. But something amazing had happened. I had slowed down my life long enough to feel it and to realize it was good. Everything was worth it. It was enough. Slowing down to Clyde's pace, I could see why he was a truly magical white horse, why he was so calm. When you slowed down to the pace of those carriage wheels slowly turning, you could see that everything you are afraid of, that you're trying daily to outrun, isn't even really there. It's a made-up cloud of stress. In actuality, when you have time to slow down and wade into it, at Clyde's pace, everything is miraculous. Realizing this, I felt elevated and refreshed, like my life finally made sense. I could see what the old people saw. And I sent up a wish.

I wished I could drive again. I wished I could do it every weekend.

Juliet Johnson

A Graceful Exit

She stood against the back wall, her head down, staring intently at the ground.

"What's the matter?" I asked, sliding the door open. She didn't acknowledge me. In the many years I had known her, she had never ignored me this way.

"Hey, Fanny girl," I said as I stepped over her untouched hay. "What's going on, sweetie?"

The twenty-one-year-old bay Arabian mare lifted her head and buried her nose softly into my outstretched hand. I patted her strong neck and ran my hand along her black mane, noting a few strands of gray hair as I did so. Her soft brown eyes locked with mine. In an instant, I felt the long-standing bond between us return. She was speaking to me without words.

Continuing to stroke her neck, I studied her huge eyes. Sounds of trotting hooves and happy cheers rose from the show ring not far from where we stood.

"What is it, girl? Too hot for you today?" I asked as I felt all around the horse's withers and girth. She felt warm, but not overly hot, which was a good sign, because the June temperatures were soaring.

Reaching down and lifting Fanny's foot, I checked for soreness. I pulled a pick from my back pocket and cleaned her hoof. Continuing with the rest of her legs, nothing looked or felt out of place. Placing my ear against her side, I heard the calming sounds of belly rumble that all horse owners listen for to ensure their horses aren't in the midst of colic. I opened her mouth and checked her gums. They were pink and healthy. She wasn't sick. She was trying to tell me something, though, something I knew had been coming, but didn't want to face.

Taking her feed bucket from its place on the wall, I turned it over and sat down. Looking closely at Fanny, I could see hints of aging, mostly gray hairs here and there. Her muscle tone, while strong and well developed, showed prominent veins in her legs and underbelly.

As I leaned back against the side of Fanny's stall, she moved toward me in a slow and deliberate manner. Her joints creaked as she carefully lifted her white-socked legs past her small manure pile in the back corner. I smiled to myself, thinking how fastidious she is for a horse. She always used the far left corner of her stall as her personal bathroom. Today was no different.

Fanny buried her warm muzzle in my hand again, wanting me to pet her nose. I did so, and our eyes met again. We sat for a long time like that, remembering the various shows we had gone to and the championships she had earned for my daughter.

My particular favorite had occurred the year before. Fanny and my daughter, Nikki, were in a bridle path hack class. The wind began to pick up as an approaching storm neared the show grounds. While the riders reversed direction and were called to a canter, a gust of wind swooped into the ring and toppled the judges' tent in the center. Of the ten entries, Fanny was the only horse who stopped and stood quietly. In my heart, I knew she had been startled, like any horse would have been. But for the protection of her best friend, Nikki, whom she loved intently, she simply came to a slow stop and stood quietly, waiting for further direction.

A year later, standing in Fanny's rented show stall, her ears were up and alert, her soft eyes inviting and loving. Sharing this quiet moment with my gentle giant brought tears to my eyes.

I had my answer. I knew what she was trying to tell me.

Fanny was tired. She was tired of horse shows and working in the blistering heat. She had been a champion mare all her life; it was in her blood. Her grandfather, the world-famous stallion, Khemosabi, had a fabulous show career. He retired several years before his death at the age of thirty-four, though he was known to sire foals past the age of thirty. Fanny was twenty-one years young, but she was tired. She, too, had earned her place in the show world.

"You're tired, aren't you, girl?" I asked, barely able to see through my mounting tears.

As if she understood my words, she answered with a deep sigh. I played with her forelock and lightly kissed the white snip that marked her dished face.

"Okay, buddy. I understand."

I slid Fanny's halter over her head, attached the lead to the ring at the bottom, and led her from the show grounds to her trailer. As she stepped into her traveling space, she turned her head and looked behind her. Cheers rose again from the show ring. Fanny nickered and swished her thick black tail, then walked to the front of the trailer so I could attach her lead to the safety latch.

The show career of Focus Fancy Love, whom we affectionately call Fanny, was over.

Betsy O'Brien Harrison

Fagan's Gifts

Home at last. Health issues had kept me apart from my family for several weeks, and I was glad to see them again. I had missed my husband, son, and daughter more than I could ever have imagined. As we caught up on hugs and news, my vivacious eight-year-old daughter, Sasheene, said she had something to show me, but it was too late to go to the paddock, so it would have to wait until tomorrow. I suspected the "something" had to do with her horse, Fagan.

At the time, we were living in a tin shed while we saved for a house. A few years prior, my children and I had been poisoned by herbicide, and we'd spent all our savings on medical treatment. Forced to sell our home and move away from pollution, we ended up on an island. The island farmers were hard-hit by drought, so paid jobs were scarce. My husband took whatever work was available, and we traded services for goods whenever possible. That was how Fagan had become part of our family.

Sasheene had ached for a horse for as long as we could remember, but horses cost money to buy and more to keep. Sadly, we simply could not afford one. Then my husband exchanged his time and skills for a seven-year-old retired racehorse.

Fagan was loved and very large. The first time Sasheene rode him, I realized I was terrified she would get injured. My fear was palpable, almost unbearable, as old memories swamped me.

It is a brilliantly sunny day. I am eight years old, and my brother and I are bareback-riding our retired racehorse, Socks. We are walking slowly along the rural road, carefree. Suddenly, a neighbor's dog bites Socks's hind leg. Naturally, he panics and bolts. My brother struggles to hold onto the reins, unable to control the huge horse, while I cling to his waist in sheer terror. The momentum is too great, though, the ride too rough, and I slide off the left side, but I'm afraid to let go, so my legs drag along the gravel road for what seems like ages. When I finally release the reins, my brother slips, too, and swings under the horse's neck, holding on for dear life. Thankfully, Sock stops immediately.

I spent months recovering from my injuries, and I was too afraid to ride again.

So it was with trepidation that I walked down our track on that brilliantly sunny day after I returned home from the hospital, following my daughter as she led Fagan across the road and into our neighbor's paddock. There, at least, the ground was firm, without the thousands of rocks that riddled our limestone fields.

"See the jumps Dad made for me?" Sasheene asked excitedly.

My heart froze.

"But you can't jump."

"Fagan can jump. I was riding him down the hill the other day, and instead of going around the bush, he just jumped right over. So Dad made these. We've been practicing—to surprise you."

Some surprise! I thought to myself, though my anxiety was clearly written all over my face. Sasheene sat me down at the end of one of the jumps. Then she calmly and firmly said, "I'll be okay, Mum. Just watch us."

Sasheene mounted Fagan and proudly walked him to the end of the paddock, all the while speaking to him lovingly. She looked so small atop the big, brown Australian Thoroughbred. I watched anxiously as she turned him and patted him encouragingly. Then, she commanded "hup," and as they began to trot toward me, I closed my eyes in fear. But hearing my daughter's laughter, I opened them again.

Sasheene was beautiful, with her hair flying out from under her riding helmet. Fagan was beautiful, too, his coat gleaming as he strode effortlessly toward the jump.

From my position on the ground, the jump towered above me and looked enormous. I shut my eyes momentarily, but forced myself to open them again. How could I tell my daughter that I had missed seeing her jump because I was afraid to see her fall?

Again, my heart stopped, but I forced myself to watch as they rose in one fluid movement and sailed high over the jump. Sasheene looked down at me, her face beaming with pride in their achievement. My heart beat again.

"See, I told you it was safe," she said. "Isn't he great? Want a ride? I won't let him take you over the jumps."

No! my mind screamed. Silently, shaking my head, I stepped back, wanting distance between me and Fagan.

"I'll just lead him with the rope," she coaxed. "You'll be safe, I promise."

It hurt to breathe. I felt sick. Gripped with fear, I could only nod in silence. I couldn't move or speak. Sasheene waited. Trembling, fighting back tears, I stood up slowly. Sasheene brought Fagan closer. The two of them stood right next to me. She told me to let Fagan smell my hand; she told him that I was her mother and I was scared. She told him she wanted him to help me not be afraid.

Time stood still—and then fell back. Once again, the childhood scene flashed before my eyes like a movie, one vivid scene after another.

My brother screams at me to let go, that I'm pulling him off. He kicks at me, trying to free himself from my death grip, and his foot strikes me in the face. The rocks rip apart my bare legs. The dog barks behind us. The horse's hooves thunder on the ground, inches from my legs. His gigantic body is taut with fear.

My own screams echo in my ears as I finally let go and fall, hard, with a jarring jolt, onto the gravel road.

I look up through the dust and my tears, and watch in horror, terrified, as my brother loses his balance and falls in front of Socks.

The pain. The blood. The screech of the ambulance siren. The X-rays. The doctor, annoyed at being called away from his golf game, saying we were stupid to be riding bareback. The pain as they pick gravel out of my legs and pour antiseptic over the wounds. The pain of rehabilitation, month upon month. The pain of trying to climb the stairs at school. The pain of kids saying I look like a mummy in the bandages. The pain when one mean girl "accidentally" bumps my leg, twice.

Terrible memories. Fagan snorted, and Sasheene laughed, breaking me out of my horrific reverie.

I looked at my daughter's face, glowing with joy and pride and love. Tears filled my eyes as I realized how close I had come to denying her this happiness . . . to preventing her from having a horse . . . to forbidding her to jump . . . to letting my fear stop her from living her dream.

I took a deep breath and stepped forward, though reluctantly. We laughed. We hugged. Then Sasheene helped me up into the saddle and proudly led her horse and her mother home, encouraging us both.

When we arrived home, she told Fagan she was going to call her father and brother to come out and see Mum. "Don't get scared when I yell."

I know he understood.

The joy on her face as she led us up to the two guys she loved dearly was a true moment of healing for me.

Fagan brought years of riding and jumping and companionship to Sasheene. Watching them together brought me happiness and brought my daughter and I even closer together. Helping groom Fagan softened my fear of horses, freeing me from the post-traumatic stress. For all those gifts, I will be forever grateful.

Marilyn Dorothea King

Clyde-Cross'd Romance

I am a horsey husband. Admittedly, I had never considered becoming such. But thanks to a crazy Clydesdale and a caring woman, that's what I've become.

When I first met Andi, I knew she was involved with horses somehow, but I didn't know the details. Within the first week of dating her, I offered to help her out at the barn, partly because I wanted to spend more time with her and get to know her, but also because I wanted to know more about horses. I had that silly thought in my head that, Hey, *if I date a horse person, I might be able to get free riding lessons.* I had never taken a riding lesson in my life, but I figured there was no time to lose.

I met Artie the first time I went to the barn with Andi. He was an 18-hand Clydesdale cross, and while my limited horse knowledge pegged him as a pinto, Andi insisted that he was a Paint. I didn't figure out until later that one was a color and the other was a breed, but in my mind it didn't really matter. Artie was white with lots of brown splotches, and that meant "pinto" to me.

What surprised me most about Artie was how goofy he was. I had never thought about horses having personalities, so seeing Artie kind of amble down the center of the barn to his stall and watching him interact with Andi was an eye-opener. I guess I should have known. I've had cats all my life, and I knew full well that every cat I'd ever lived with or met had a personality of its own. It just didn't occur to me that horses would be the same.

As I said, Artie was a goofy horse. He had that type of demeanor and personality that you just sort of fall in love with. If he were a person, I guess he'd be the kid in school who wasn't the brightest and wasn't the dumbest but was the one who somehow ended up being friends with everyone without making an effort.

Artie was also completely oblivious as to how big he was, and he had a tendency to plow into people and through fences without really realizing what he was doing. He didn't intentionally break things, but when he leaned his considerable mass on you, you knew it.

The first couple of weeks I helped Andi at the barn, I learned how to clean stalls, which I likened to standing in a huge litter box with a rake instead of cleaning out a box with a pooper-scooper. Because I cleaned the stall with Artie in it while he ate his feed, I quickly learned that I needed nimble feet in there. He had a tendency to shift around in his stall as he ate, and I doubt he would have noticed if he had crushed his stall cleaner against the wall.

In addition to learning how to pick and prepare stalls, I learned how to drop feed and hay, pick Artie's feet, and understand the basics of the ground work for horsemanship. I was also learning how important Artie was to Andi. I could see how her mood changed when she got to the barn, how grooming Artie would calm her down after a long day at work, and how just going through the list of barn-related chores brought a sense of peace, a sense of belonging to her.

Some days I'd go to the barn with Andi to help out, but other days she preferred to go to the barn herself, no doubt seeking out that special connection between her and Artie that I had only really gotten a glimpse of. Somewhere during that first month of dating, I realized that the horse-rider connection was something that would be with her for the rest of her life, that if I were to continue my relationship with Andi, I'd be sharing her to some extent with Artie and any future horses that came along. Horses were very important to Andi, and I knew I'd never ask her to make a choice between them and me. But it was something I knew I'd have to think about.

With that on my mind, I joined Andi on a barn trip one day about a month into our relationship, and we discovered that Artie, true to form, had pushed his way through the top rail of the weather-beaten fence surrounding his paddock. As we approached his paddock, we noticed the broken pieces of boards all over the place. Artie stood near the paddock gate with his usual goofy expression on his face, as if he were saying, "Hullo, Mom and Dad."

Andi led Artie to the barn so that he could be fed, and I started picking up the broken boards and repairing the busted fence. A new board and a few banged-in nails later, the fence repair was finished, and I joined Andi in the barn. She was in Artie's stall, and I noticed she was spending a lot of time under his head, working on his chest.

I saw blood running down from where she was working, so I asked what had happened. She glanced at me with an unhappy expression and told me that Artie had a splinter in his chest. I've had splinters in my fingers before, so I didn't really understand the problem—surely it was just a little bit of wood that a pair of tweezers could get out.

Andi couldn't get the splinter out, so we gave the veterinarian a call. As we waited for him to show up, we finished all the other barn chores and took care of Artie, though he was oblivious to our concern, content to hang out in his stall and accept the cookies and treats I gave him.

The vet arrived and went to work on Artie. Much to my surprise, the vet ended up digging more than four inches worth of wood splinters out of Artie's chest. Clearly, Artie had been lucky he hadn't killed himself on the fence. With the wood out, Artie was left with a strangely shaped hole in his chest, almost like a second mouth. The vet gave Andi a big intravenous bag of saline and some care instructions, then left.

The next day, Andi and I went to the barn to do the usual chores, and Andi needed help taking care of Artie's wound. I volunteered, thinking in the back of my mind that I might be in this for the long haul. As I stood there in the stall, holding up the IV bag and watching Andi irrigate Artie's wound with the IV and her hand, I confirmed that thought and realized that I loved Andi and I loved Artie.

I jokingly asked Andi if horse care ever got much worse than what we were doing now, with the IV and fingers plunged deep into Artie's seeping chest wound, and she remarked that this was probably close to the top of the list of disgusting but necessary activities that came with horse care and ownership.

I thought about that over the next day or two, but my mind was set. Andi was a caring soul with a lot of love in her heart, and I knew that no matter where we went or what happened, I'd be happy being with her and sharing her life with horses.

I proposed to Andi, kneeling in the farrier stall of the barn. She said yes, Artie's chest wound healed fully, and my life as a horse spouse, a good groom, and an outstanding cookie and treat dispenser began in full. I have the chest wound of a gentle but goofy pinto and the love and care of his rider to thank for it, and I couldn't be happier about it.

Jim Johnson

Mooney and Me

We drove down the road in silence. My dad's movements were sharp as he shifted gears. He was angry. It probably wasn't because of me, but that didn't matter. He'd find something wrong with me as an excuse to lash out. I sat perfectly still and fixed my gaze outside the passenger window. Just a few more minutes.

Our old Festiva rattled noisily. The car was one of dad's "good deals." The previous owner had customized it into a convertible. But the top didn't really fit and barely stayed put when pulled up. Mom always gave a disapproving look when she saw Dad take it out. She'd probably kill him if she knew he was driving me around in it now. They were in a heated argument right before we left. Finances were really tight, and the stress made my dad prone to angry outbursts at any given moment.

The stable's driveway came into view. I held my breath. My right knuckles were white from clutching the door handle. I pressed my forehead to the window. There was still a minute left for the angry words to start flowing. The car bounced and jostled over the potholes and gravel, then came to a stop. My dad let the engine idle as he waited for me to get out. He didn't look at me. I could see his jaw tightening and releasing as he ground his teeth. I climbed out and then poked my head back in.

"My lesson ends at noon," I said.

"Yeah, I know. I'll be here."

He shifted into first. I stepped back quickly and shut the door. He'd probably be late picking me up. He always was. Often, he'd forget me completely. There was a time when he was interested in my life. But not anymore. It was only at mom's insistence that he bothered to drive me to the stable. A lump built in my throat as I watched him drive off. I tried to assure myself that it was because he was under a lot of stress. A tear escaped. I blinked back another. I swallowed hard and wiped my eyes clear with my fist. I took a deep breath, and the smell of horses filled my lungs. I closed my eyes for a moment and let the smell clear my head. Then I turned and hurried to the barn.

The other students were already busy grooming and saddling. Trish, the instructor, was helping a little girl in brand new pink boots and a flashy rhine-stone-studded T-shirt get her saddle onto the back of the buckskin named Houdini. If left to himself, the old horse would have his halter off in about ten minutes. He was a gentleman, though. I walked up timidly, self-conscience of my worn out clothes and hand-me-down boots. Finances being what they were, my parents couldn't afford to buy me any riding gear. I was just grateful they hadn't cut out my riding lessons completely. I clung to my new helmet, a Christmas present from my aunt. Before, I had used one of the old helmets kept on hand for students who came to lessons without their own. They were none too clean and most of them too big.

Trish looked up and saw me. "Hey! Just a minute, and I'll show you which horse you're to ride today."

I waited quietly and watched another girl brush down the palomino horse I had been riding. He had been a fun challenge for me. The big horse was very gentle and compliant most of the time. But he was lazy. He was more interested in food than riding. I looked around and saw all the other lesson horses out and paired with students and wondered what my instructor had in mind. Trish finished helping the little girl with her saddle.

"Okay. Come on."

Trish led me about halfway down the barn, then stopped in front of a stall. It was too high for me to see in. I craned my neck anyway and nearly sprained my thumbs fiddling with my helmet as I waited. She pushed open the door and grabbed the halter hanging on the hook to the left of it. She stepped in, and I followed.

"This is Mooney. I got her just this week."

The horse was a small chestnut mare with a large white star on her forehead. Her large, dark eyes seemed sort of sad and wary. Trish calmly approached her and gently slipped on the halter. Mooney's head raised and stiffened, and her eyes bulged.

"She's come from a very bad home. You'll have to be careful with her, but I think you can handle it. With a little patience and love, she'll learn to trust you."

The sound of the other student's chatting vanished. My old, worn-out clothes were forgotten. The little bit of lump left in my throat went unnoticed. Mooney engulfed my whole attention. Trish led her out of the stall and to the front of the tack room, where everyone else was almost finished saddling. My eyes stayed fixed on Mooney. Instead of tying her to the hitching rail like the rest of the horses, Trish held on to Mooney's lead rope.

"Go ahead and start brushing her," she said.

Trish explained that the last owner had beat Mooney while she was tied at a hitching rail and now she was afraid to be tied. I became lost in the task of brushing the little mare. I talked soothingly to her as I brushed, telling her that everything was going to be fine now. As I ran my hand along her neck and shoulders, I could feel the tightness of her muscles. She was nervous, ready to bolt at any moment. Each time I removed my hand or brush and replaced it, she jumped slightly. The tension in my own arms relaxed. I wanted her to feel safe when I touched her. I wanted to tell her I was a friend.

"Okay," Trish said. "Go get a saddle. Just be careful putting it on her. She's very jumpy."

I followed her instructions. Mooney danced sideways as I lifted the saddle over my head and toward her back. Trish talked to her and stroked her, and she stood still again.

"Try again. Gently now."

I lifted the saddle and strained every muscle in my body to keep from dropping it down too suddenly on her back. Mooney shifted her feet nervously, but she stood.

"Now, be very careful with the cinch. Don't tighten it up right away. Let her calm down first, and then we'll tighten it up a little at a time."

I did as I was told. Trish handed me the bridle she had assembled for Mooney. I reached over Mooney's head and slid it over her face. She paused a moment before opening her mouth for the bit. Then I pulled the bridle the rest of the way over her ears. She closed her eyes protectively. She was still tense and nervous. But she was compliant.

"She didn't fight you with the bridle. That's a good sign. We'll be able to help her yet."

I led Mooney to the arena, where the other students were already warming up. Trish followed behind me.

"I'll hold her while you mount up. She'll be fine once you start walking. Make a couple rounds of the arena and then finish tightening your cinch."

When I settled into the saddle, I could feel the intense nervousness shivering through Mooney's body. I picked up the reigns tenderly and let all the love and comfort I could find within myself flow through my fingers.

"That's a good girl, Mooney. Easy now. Let's walk." I cued her forward, and she stepped out anxiously. I gently urged her on and then calmly settled into her swinging rhythm. I talked to her softly. She slowly began to relax as we went. After a couple rounds of the arena, I stopped and tightened her cinch as my instructor had said.

"Okay, girls, pick up the trot," Trish said.

The two-hour lesson seemed to go by within minutes. With a reluctance greater than I had ever felt before, I dismounted. I brushed Mooney down, standing as close to her as I could and keeping one hand on her at all times. I wanted to melt into her, become part of her. I talked constantly to her, softly. Her entire body relaxed, and her ears twitched back and forth at the sound of my voice. I put her back in her stall and lingered to watch her. The usually torturous minutes waiting and wondering if my dad would show passed unnoticed. I almost didn't hear his honking horn.

The next week, I was deaf to my dad's angry ranting and raving. All I could think of was Mooney. The drive from my home to the stable seemed longer than ever. My knee bounced up and down impatiently at each stop light. Our bumpy pace over the stable's driveway seemed agonizingly slow. The car had barely come to a halt when I jumped out, and I almost forgot to remind my dad what time to pick me up. I rushed to the barn. My heart caught in my throat when I reached Mooney's stall. Mooney was already out and being held by one of the other students! *It's okay!* I told myself. *Just talk to Trish.* I quickly located her. I didn't even have to ask my question.

"Yes! You get to ride Mooney. You can ride her from now on, until I say differently."

I breathed a sigh of relief. Mooney's ear pricked when I approached; she was glad to see me too.

From then on, Mooney looked for me every Saturday and nickered to me when I came in view. As the weeks went by, her trust in me grew and grew. After a while, she no longer cared if I tied her to the hitching post. As long as I warned her that the cinch was coming by firmly rubbing her belly, she would let me cinch her up without a fuss.

Mooney and I had something special. We understood each other. We felt each other's pain. During the week, while I was at home or elsewhere, just thinking of her gave me refuge. On the days when my dad said something particularly hurtful, Mooney would push those words from my mind.

I rode Mooney for several years. She introduced me to the world of gymkhana and even brought me several blue ribbons. I cried the day she was sold. Though she went to a good home, I wondered if her new owner would be able to connect with her as I had. I wondered if she would miss me as much as I would miss her. She pulled me through some of the darkest moments of my childhood. In each other, we found hope and healing. Together, we learned that trust and love grow in the circle of kindness.

Terri Hardison

Rebel with a Cause

Drumming my fingers on the steering wheel, I waited for the flag girl to wave me through. *This is Wyoming*, I thought. *There's always road construction here; I might as well just sit back and relax.* I rolled down the car window, took a deep breath of spring air, and let my gaze drift across the field bordering the highway. Stunned by what I saw, I missed the flag girl's wave to proceed. There, standing like a vision, was the most beautiful Paint I had ever seen.

I love horses. I've always loved horses. As a horse-crazy young girl, I'd dream of horses every night and daydream about horses every day. Although I was raised in a small city and didn't have a horse of my own, my grandparents were only one state away and owned a ranch with horses. So I'd learned to ride, after a fashion, but I'd never learned the different riding disciplines or even how to properly care for a horse. That night, after spotting the Paint in the field, I again dreamed of horses—well, one horse in particular.

On my way home from work the next day, I stopped at the ranch house and asked the owner about the wonderful horse I'd seen.

"That's just old Rebel." She explained that at one time Rebel had been ranked fifth in the nation as a barrel racer on the rodeo circuit. When he retired from that, they had used him as a packhorse to carry game trophies for their guided hunting parties. "As you can see, his back is shot as a result of his years of barrel racing and hunting duties. He's only nine years old, but I imagine we'll have to put him down soon. He's just no use to us any more," she said.

So I bought him. What else could I do?

Now what? Since I lived in town, I needed a place to pasture Rebel. *No problem,* I thought. About three miles from my home, by Sinks Canyon, is a beautiful horse facility. I made a quick call, and, fortunately, they had an opening for one more horse. It was perfect—the best hay, stalls for when the weather turned cold, both indoor and outdoor arenas, plus 2,000 acres for trail riding. I had a horse, and he had a home.

I discovered a few slight drawbacks with Rebel's new home, though. The other horses kept at the facility were Thoroughbreds; most of them cost more than many people earned in a year. Plus, the other owners could actually ride. In fact, two of the ladies had represented the United States in the Olympics. In other words, Rebel and I didn't exactly fit in.

I did everything I could to improve the situation. I read and watched anything I could find on riding and caring for horses. I went to the ranch in the evenings, when no one was around, to practice riding. Rebel didn't mind, and he calmly did his best to teach me to ride. Although he sometimes seemed to question why he was the one doing the teaching, he remained patient with me. Still, despite all of my efforts to blend in, I became known as "the woman with the old, fat, ugly Paint horse." Rebel and I were way out of our league!

One evening while I was riding indoors and feeling discouraged, another owner, Sally, arrived. I quickly decided to put Rebel back in the field so I wouldn't embarrass myself with my lack of riding skills. As I was walking him back, Sally's eight-year-old daughter ran over to Rebel. It was love at first sight—to Sally's shock. She had been trying for several years to share her love of horses with her daughter, but the young girl had refused—until that moment—to have anything to do with horses. Now, she was begging for a ride.

"You've got a special horse there," Sally said, and a friendship was born.

Sally started giving me riding lessons and working with Rebel. In return, I let her daughter ride him. After a while, Sally began to notice how Rebel behaved around children—all children—and how sweet he was with me, a novice rider. It gave her an idea. Sally called her friend Carol, and things began to change.

Carol worked with the Wyoming State School, and at Sally's urging she came out to meet Rebel. It didn't take long for Carol to recognize that Rebel had the special something they had been looking for in a horse. She knew that with proper training he could be a real asset for the school. So Rebel began his third, and perhaps most important, career.

Every Tuesday for several months, Carol came to the horse facility with eight special children. They all loved, patted, and rode Rebel—all, that is, but one. Twelve-year-old Linda had autism, a disorder that inhibited her ability to communicate and socialize. Linda didn't laugh or cry, and she seldom spoke. At the arena, she always sat in a corner by herself, watching but never joining in.

One day Rebel apparently decided this had gone on long enough. He walked right up to Linda and put his big old nose in her face, as if to say, "Why don't you want to ride me?"

Linda stood up and began to pat Rebel. Carol quietly motioned Linda's parents, who had been waiting by the bus, to come closer and observe this unbelievable event. Then something even more amazing happened . . . Linda smiled. As though a smile wasn't enough for him, though, Rebel—who was always up for a good rump rub—turned around and presented his backside to Linda. For one of the first times in her life, Linda laughed out loud.

Carol walked up to Linda and asked gently, "Would you like to ride?"

Linda nodded her head. Carol helped her mount and led her around the arena. After a few laps, she handed the reigns to Linda, who guided the big horse at a walk by herself. Linda laughed out loud the entire time she rode. When it was time to dismount, she walked around to the front of the horse, kissed Rebel on the nose, and said, "I love you."

Tears welled up in the eyes of all who had witnessed the incredible exchange between Linda and Rebel. For the next year, every Tuesday, an excited Linda arrived to spend time with her special friend. And though other horses were brought over for the children to enjoy, Linda only had eyes, and smiles, for Rebel.

Eventually, Linda's family moved away, but one of the first things they did after settling into their new home was to find a horse that Linda could love and buy it. Now, Linda rides daily, and as she rides, she continues to express the joy that is often trapped inside her—thanks to a horse who taught her how to smile.

Word quickly spread about Rebel's special bond with children and about his work with special-needs kids. He was no longer known as the "old, fat, ugly Paint." Indeed, he became the most popular horse on the ranch. He had a cause for living.

But for this Rebel, one cause wasn't enough. He had one more person who needed to be nudged by his big old nose. Once, I had rescued him from being put down and started him on a new career. Now, he returned the favor. Inspired by his example, I gathered my courage and left my city job. Today, I do what I've always dreamed of doing: I work at a stable, exercising horses all day, everyday.

Rebel's back condition has slowly worsened over time. These days, he is limited to friends patting, rather than riding, but loving hands are always available. Never again will the question of his life being over arise, because there will always be someone who needs Rebel's unique brand of love and gentleness. And he will always meet their needs—head, or rump, on.

Lesa Cameron, as told by Tammy Lewis

Mirror, Mirror in the Stall

My heart raced with excitement as the wheels of the horse trailer crunched on the gravel. Vida, my new mare, had just arrived at the barn where I would board her. Her former owner, Judy, backed her from the trailer, each of Vida's slender hind legs reaching tentatively for the ground.

"Easy, girl, easy," Judy clucked and soothed as she led my quarter horse/Arabian beauty in a large circle before me.

I couldn't believe my good fortune. The ad for Vida was the first I'd seen when I shopped for a horse, a childhood dream come true. I'd taken one look at her intelligent face, alert ears, and broad white blaze down her chestnut muzzle, and searched no further. She was gorgeous. Plus, the ad had promised she was a push-button horse, one that would do what the rider asked immediately and with only the slightest of cues. Exactly right for me. I'd taken some riding lessons and ridden a few times with a friend who coached me on everything from bits to fly spray, but this was my first experience boarding my own horse.

Judy handed me Vida's lead rope with a teary sniff. "I can't feel too bad leaving her here. She'll be in horse heaven," she said, surveying the twenty acres of pasture that would be Vida's new playground. Eight horses in groups of two and three looked up from their grazing to see the new kid on the block. In the mottled shade of two big pines, a palomino standing a good 16 hands leaned close to a much smaller bay mare. A white and brown Appaloosa stood guard over a dappled gray who lifted his head to regard Vida, then returned to his snoozing in the sun. A slim white horse that I guessed to be an Arabian, a chestnut that might be Vida's twin but stockier, and a big sway-backed black horse that had to be at least thirty years old nibbled grass near the white fence. These would be Vida's new friends.

"Do you need anything else?" Judy asked, one foot in the cab of her truck, as she turned for a last look at Vida and me.

"I think we're fine, thanks." I held Vida's lead rope where it snapped to the halter, as Judy had done, and talked quietly to her as we watched the trailer pull away. "You'll like it here," I said, stroking her shoulder. "I promise."

Vida stood in place for another minute or two, and then began to toss her head. She lifted one front leg and pawed the air.

I moved her forward, leading her in a circle, mimicking Judy's actions.

Vida's sedate walk turned into a nervous dance. She no longer circled, but stuck her nose out and pranced a jagged line down the gravel driveway. Every time she tossed her head she amped up my fear along with hers. I'd heard that horses and owners mirror each other. The theory was certainly holding true for us.

I loosened the lead rope, backing away from possible flailing hooves and bared teeth. If Vida were a push-button horse, where was the "calm" button? Her nostrils flared, her ears flicked forward and back, and her eyes were ringed with white.

Running alongside her, I somehow pulled enough on the lead rope to bring her around toward the barn. "It's okay, girl," I said. But my voice cracked. She knew it wasn't okay.

I looked around for help. *Where were the other boarders? Why had I told the barn owner to show me Vida's stall and I would be fine moving her in alone?* At Vida's former home I'd ridden her several times and she'd been mild-mannered in every way. I simply hadn't considered that bringing her to a new place would upset her so much.

The part of my brain not yet frozen with terror tried to think what to do. Surely I had read or heard of some advice for a moment like this. The only thing my sputtering brain could come up with was, "Show them who's boss." Apparently Vida had been given the same advice, and she was showing me all right.

An image from the film *The Black Stallion* made its way into my mind: a boy standing absolutely still, holding out his hand to the stallion, murmuring soft words of comfort as the horse reared and plunged— and the black stallion quieting, accepting the boy's touch. No novel lesson in horse handling there, but much easier to watch on film than to actually do. Despite being a lot older than that boy, I didn't have half his guts.

Vida snorted and trotted faster. Sweat glistened on her coat. I felt my own perspiration damp under my arms. From somewhere deep in my left toe, I mustered enough willpower to slow my pace and steady my voice. "You're okay, girl. I know everything is new and strange. I don't know what I'm doing here either."

I fully extended the lead rope so that it became a short lounge line. Standing still and facing Vida's side, I murmured, "Easy, girl, easy." Slowly, her erratic path became a circle. My heart still pounded, but I kept up a stream of encouraging words as I gently tugged the lead rope. "Walk, Vida. Good girl. Slow and easy. Whoa now. Whoa."

Vida slowed to a walk, then stopped and faced me, though she trembled. My knees still weak, my breath still tight in my chest, I held out my hand as the boy had done. Though Vida didn't walk to me and nuzzle me with her whiskered nose, her eyes softened. My chest expanded with relief, and I drew a deep breath. I reached out to pat her sweat-stained shoulder. The calming button seemed to be my own state of being. Once again, we mirrored each other.

Vida's anxiety didn't disappear right away, nor did mine. Those first days with her I often spent forty-five frantic minutes in the pasture, trying to catch my nervous mare as I worked both of us into a lather. But over the next few weeks, some kind of equine magic began to settle over me. No matter what my state of mind when I left home, a sense of well being would rise in me, relaxing my knotted shoulders and quieting my jumbled mind, as I drove along the fenced pasture, admiring my lovely horse. I would park and put on my barn boots, take a carrot or apple from the passenger seat along with Vida's halter, and slip between the white vinyl slats of the fence. Time seemed to slow down as I stood before Vida, buckling on her halter and running my fingers through the burnished red hair of her forelock. The quieter I became, the more quickly she relaxed.

Over the next few weeks, I learned that her waving foreleg meant "help." She might have a scrape or a nip from horse games in the pasture that needed some healing salve and kisses, or she might need me to croon words of comfort when a horse buddy left for a new home. In turn, she would swing her head around and gently push my shoulder as I brushed her broad flanks or combed her mane and tail while I poured out all my worries.

Vida and I moved on to ground work. When I enlisted the help of a trainer/instructor, we quickly saw that Vida had problems trotting comfortably. I called a chiropractor recommended by another boarder, a big man in a plaid shirt and jeans who had worked on his own horses and others for thirty years. He quickly inspired my confidence by the way he talked to Vida as he stroked her neck and sides, building her trust before he began his work. Then he made a number of small adjustments in her hips, along her back, and in her shoulders and neck. Vida visibly relaxed under his hands.

The chiropractor showed me exercises to do with her every time I came to the barn to strengthen her back and keep it aligned. "I find that if a horse hurts somewhere, the owner usually does too," he said as he stretched one of Vida's forelegs and held it, waiting for a release. "You might want to think about that."

That mirror image thing again. But wasn't mirrored body pain going a bit too far? I wasn't prepared to call a chiropractor for myself. Yet, I had to admit to chronic lower back pain. His words haunted me till I got my own adjustment and enrolled in yoga classes. I was amazed how much better I felt when I did a yoga home practice daily.

Vida's back and mine grew stronger, and it was time to hit the trails. I'd borrowed a treeless saddle, one designed to fit any horse, for the little riding Vida and I had done. The equine world abounded with horror stories of damage done to horses by poorly fitting saddles. I described Vida's conformation to the owner of a local tack shop who specialized in saddle fit, and she suggested half a dozen used saddles she had that might work. I piled them in my car and drove to the barn. Each time I set one on Vida's back she snapped her head around and bared her teeth. Apparently they all pinched or rubbed. I returned the saddles and brought out another half dozen. Vida wouldn't tolerate any of them either.

I fumed all the way back to the tack store. *Had I made my horse hypersensitive with all the body work?* The owner reassured me that, indeed, it could take more than a dozen saddles to find a proper fit and offered to come out to the barn. After seeing Vida she suggested three more saddles. Unfortunately, they were all new. She had nothing similar in a used saddle.

Dollar signs spun in my head. I looked down at the worn cuffs of my barn jacket, the single pair of riding pants I had purchased and already mended in two places, the scuffed, mud-caked toes of my worn boots. This time Vida and I were definitely not mirror images. I did not require the best clothes in town.

Back at the barn, I settled a particularly soft leather dressage saddle on Vida's back. She stood quietly, instead of snapping her head around, and pricked her ears forward as if to say, "This is it, let's go." The difference in her attitude astounded me. Okay, so we'd found a saddle that fit. I could have advertised and found the same saddle used, except it was a new model that Steuben had put out just that year. I thought of my credit card bill, then sighed and buckled the girth. I had only a few pair of shoes, but I had certainly bought them new, and they had tended to be expensive because comfort and expense seem to go together.

In the five years I've had Vida, we've learned to read each other's body signals and sometimes, it seems, each other's minds. We like the same trails and dislike the same repetitious arena work, though we discipline ourselves to do it. We have the same favorite people and horses at the barn. She has truly become a push-button horse. After all, we are mirror images and understand each other a little better every day.

Samantha Ducloux Waltz

King of My Heart

The slightly sway-backed older Paint seemed to my mom to be an ideal first horse for a nine-year-old girl. We'd driven by his ranch many times and seen the painted gelding with a white "map" of North America splashed across his left side grazing in the field, always mellow and easy going. So when the "Horse for Sale—$100" sign went up, Mom took me with her to check him out.

Though I'd never had my own horse, I'd been a horse girl since I was five. Mom had grown up on a farm in Kansas with a horse of her own, and she remembered the endless hours of joy she'd spent riding Pony Pet across the vast fields. She wanted me to have similar memories. Though we didn't live on a farm, our place in the country fit the bill.

Another horse regularly grazed in the field with the Paint: a red-eyed albino who often had pinned-back ears and high-kicking heels. Mom and I hoped it was the peaceful Paint and not the wild albino for sale. Lucky for me, it was. Aptly named Diablo ("devil"), the albino didn't appeal to me. But the good-natured gelding was perfect. Even his regal name, El Rey—"the king"—was perfect, for he became the king of my heart, a noble knight who would carry me through rough times.

After introductions and a general look-over, I led El Rey through the grassy field. He strode easily beside me, rubbing his nose in my long hair, snuffling it and blowing strands into my face. I loved him instantly.

The owner offered to saddle him up, but I asked to ride him around bareback with just the halter. Being a shorty, I needed a leg up, which the owner gladly provided. The gelding stood there patiently as I tried to find a comfortable spot on his bony back. Fortunately, his gait was smoother than his back. We got along famously, jogging around the field.

The ranch house was on one side of the highway, and the large pasture was on the other, accessed through a gate and an underpass. While Mom chatted with the owners on the porch, El Rey and I ventured toward the far end of the field and found the underpass. The click-click sounds of cars speeding along the freeway above didn't faze the old guy as we clip-clopped along.

We trotted up a little hill, and there before us was an expanse of rolling pasture, gleaming golden green in the sunlight. El Rey sniffed the fresh air, surveyed the grassy hills, danced a bit, trotted, and then headed out at a full gallop! Maybe he sought his mates around the curve of the hill. Maybe he just wanted to stretch his long legs. Whatever the reason, he seemed to run with purpose and glee. For my part, I proudly held my seat, thighs squeezing tightly and fists gripping his mane. It took me a few minutes, but I reined him in.

When El Rey finally trotted to a stop atop a hill overlooking the pasture, the highway, and his barn, he snorted with delight, tossed his head, and turned back to me, nudging my toe as if to say, "Wasn't that fun?" Indeed it was! Because as much as I wanted a horse that wouldn't toss me on a whim, I also wanted one with some spunk. El Rey was both.

We rode around the pasture for a while, getting to know one another. I dismounted and walked with him, then found a boulder to help me back up. He stood still, the perfect gentleman. In fact, he was always a gentleman. It's worth noting that in all the years El Rey was my equine companion, the only time he "ran away" with me was that first time I rode him.

When we returned to the ranch house, Mom was sharing iced tea with the owners. Before long, the deal was cinched up, and El Rey was mine.

"He's a fine one, this horse," the owner said, rubbing the Paint's forehead. "Got a good spirit."

El Rey's spirit remained good for many years. He made himself quite at home at our house in the Ojai village. We had a big, grassy front yard dotted with trees, and El Rey kept the grass nicely cropped—which my two older brothers appreciated, since it virtually eliminated their need to mow it. We stored tack in a breezeway near the corral. El Rey often wandered in there around dinner time. He'd push open the top half of the split double door and stick his head into the kitchen. Mom usually had fresh carrots for him.

I'm not sure if Mom really knew what a positive force that large, hoofed companion was in my life. He very likely saved me, too, during those tumultuous years for our family. My parents had difficulties in their marriage, and eventually they broke up. On top of that, my brothers got into some major teenage trouble, after they started running with some bad kids who were involved with drugs. Fortunately, they came through it and are now fine adult men.

Mom always tried to protect us kids from life's unpleasant experiences. Her job was made easier with me because of my painted companion. El Rey and I spent hours together after school and on weekends. He was my transport away from problems and into a world of imagination and happiness. Any weekend we could be seen clip-clopping along the tree-lined lanes, my hair flowing in warm breezes fragrant with citrus and eucalyptus. Down by the wooded creek we could find a safe adventure and cool off during hot summer days. I loved the deep pool, where we'd wade in up to his withers—bareback, of course! I'd slide off and paddle around the water. Mom never worried about me on those days; I'd always tell her where I was headed as I packed some food and water for me and carrots for El Rey. And being with El Rey made me feel safe.

I had a vivid, lively imagination. Sometimes I was an Indian guide leading settlers to a new land. Other days I might be a movie star riding incognito through the British Isles. Other times, I was just me, happy me, temporarily carried away from the problems at home. Always, I traveled with my beloved companion, El Rey.

Looking back now, I realize that I, too, could have fallen into trouble. The soil was fertile for it. But being with and caring for El Rey kept me busy and even insulated me somewhat from my family's problems. My fantasy life while riding El Rey not only provided a way for my subconscious to protect me from the turmoil happening around me, it also helped shape me into the writer I am today. A writer needs a rich imagination, and my role-playing on the back of El Rey honed my ability to create characters, scenes, and dialogue. I'm sure those experiences also contributed to my lifelong tendency to look for the silver lining in any situation, no matter how dark it might seem.

There were other silver linings, too. Although times were tough, the picture wasn't all black and bleak. My brothers and I made some great memories together in Ojai—especially Paul, who shares my love of horses. When Mom got him a lively mare named Nachee, the times he and I spent together with our horses formed a bond that lasts to this day.

Whereas El Rey was calm and collected, Nachee was his opposite. The lovely, chestnut Arab was too much for me to handle, but Paul, who is four years my senior, had the magic touch. The pair was a hit at local horse shows. Paul would groom Nachee until her coat shone and her mane and tail were silky smooth. While Paul and Nachee were experts in the equestrian classes, El Rey and I could cut through the pole bending and keyhole events with barely a whisper on the poles. My Paint wasn't always the fastest horse, but he was nimble of hoof, and I could keep my legs in tight so as not to knock down any poles. We took our share of ribbons.

But neither of those events ended up being his glory. Where El Rey shined the most was in the Grand Entry. The Grand Entry of our country shows was the event in which all the riders could strut their stuff. It also had the best ribbons! More open in format than the classes, it was a fun way to end the show, and the riders tried to impress the judges with grandeur and cleverness. A sparkly silver saddle that was too heavy for racing, a girl dressed in Arabian scarves fluttering in the breeze, even trick riding found their way into the Grand Entry.

Paul usually took an elegant approach, prancing into the arena in his smooth dress chaps and brushed hat, with Nachee's tail held high and ears perked up. Sometimes I'd dress as an Indian guide on my bareback Paint. We took a different tack the year El Rey claimed his fame as master of the Grand Entry.

You see, El Rey loved Nachee. He was smitten. He'd nuzzle her mane, nicker when she was out, and follow her around whenever they were together. So one day Paul and I found a way to capitalize on my gelding's affection for his Arab sweetheart.

The Grand Entry event was paced in a way that allowed everyone to enter and get their due from the audience. Flag bearers came first, followed by the entrants. Knowing El Rey would gladly follow Nachee wherever Paul rode her, we took the last two positions in line and put our show stopper into motion.

After all the others had made their entrance, Paul road in, looking as sharp as a cowboy could, atop his gorgeous Arabian. The audience applauded as he pranced up to the judges and tipped his hat. As Paul started his circle around the arena, the announcer called out his name. Then Paul and Nachee ducked behind the other horses.

A moment later, the announcer's voice was heard again, "Wait a minute. Excuse me, miss!"

All eyes turned to the gate, where El Rey and I were entering. El Rey jogged in, then paused and turned his head, looking for his lady love. I was sitting backward, bent over his bare rump. No halter, no bridle, no pad, nothing.

"Are you lost?" called the announcer.

I didn't reply, because I was deep in concentration, leaning on my elbows, peering at a map spread across El Rey's rump.

El Rey nickered and then started cruising around the arena, searching for his heart's desire. I looked up to get my bearings and then pointed a finger at the map.

"May we help you?" came the announcer's voice again, reverberating overhead.

I looked at the announcer and pantomimed pointing here and there, looking at the map, tossing my hands up in confusion.

Meanwhile, Paul jogged around the arena, weaving in and out of where the others were standing. By then, El Rey had spotted Nachee and was dutifully following her path, narrowing the gap between them. The audience roared and applauded as we made a circuit around the other riders. Finally, I referenced my map again and with large gestures pantomimed "Aha!" Then I turned around to face forward and nudged my steed to our place next to Paul and Nachee at the end of the line. When the applause wound down, the judges strode forward with our big blue ribbon. They gave us the red, too, for being so entertaining.

Although the ribbons and even the horses have long since disappeared, the memory will always be close to my heart—along with many others of my king, my confidant, my painted champion, El Rey.

Sheina North

A Love Affair to Remember

Most teenage girls love horses. At one time in my life I found it hard to understand the attraction.

"Do you want to go with me tomorrow to feed my horse? I'll let you ride him," my friend Nancy offered after a long day of bumping elbows at our crowded junior high school.

"Um, I guess." I hesitated. "Yeah, I'll go."

I was not an outdoorsy sort of girl. My experience with horses was watching the Lone Ranger and Tonto dash across my parents' black-and-white TV screen. But Nancy was my best friend, and I loved being with her, so I just went along for the ride.

I was completely unprepared for the experience. Wearing my white tennis shoes, I climbed into the saddle with Nancy's help. I held tightly to the saddle horn while she led her horse around in a circle, and then I bounced up and down when she urged him into a trot. I helped brush his shining sorrel coat and curry his dark red mane, pulling the cockle burrs out of his coarse tail. When I scooped pungent feed into a plastic bucket, I fought to stay upright as Nancy's horse hungrily shoved in his nose.

That was all it took: I was in love. When I got home, I announced to my parents that I was buying a horse.

"A horse?" my mother asked. "Where are you going to keep it?"

"I don't know. I guess we'll have to find a stable nearby."

"In suburban Dallas?" my dad questioned.

"Yeah. Maybe I can keep it where Nancy keeps her horse."

"Do you have any idea how much it will cost to buy a horse? Feed a horse? Buy a saddle and all the stuff you need to ride and take care of a horse?" Dad said.

"No, but I have some money saved from my birthdays, and I'll sell my piano."

"The piano? You're kidding! I thought you loved playing the piano," my mother said.

"Yes, but I love riding more. I want to sell the piano and use the money to pay for a horse. I really do. Please, can we put an ad in the newspaper right away?"

And sell the piano I did.

The next problem was my boyfriend.

"I don't want you to get a horse. If you get a horse, you won't have any time for me," he complained. "You'll have to choose: me or a horse."

He was a nice-enough guy, but after carefully considering the matter for about five minutes, I said, "Okay, I choose the horse."

"The horse?" He was shocked.

"Yes, I want the horse. Sorry. Bye." I hung up the phone.

My love affair with Jesse, a seven-year-old bay gelding, began the instant I saw him. Something in his eyes, in the way he stood solidly before me—calm and strong, yet curious, sniffing my boots and hair, slobbering on my plaid shirt and jeans—told me that this was a horse I could count on to carry me safely through whatever lay ahead.

With the money from the sale of the piano, plus my savings, I bought Jesse and a used saddle, a used bridle, a new saddle blanket and pad, assorted hoof picks, curry brushes, buckets, a pair of boots, and a barrel to store feed in. I read every single book our local library had on horses. I took out a year's subscription to *American Quarter Horse Journal*.

I found a stable near our house and a ride to get to and from the stable when my mother couldn't take me. I rode Jesse every day, trotting around the practice arena, galloping through the 100-acre pasture, or cantering to the nearby lake and around the golf course. As we rode up and down the grassy highway shoulders, I steadied Jesse with a careful pat on the neck whenever a passing car honked "hello."

I threw myself into play days and rodeos and 4-H club. I even loved the barn's aroma of sweaty horses mixed with hay and manure. At a local crafts fair, my friend Nancy bought a wood-burned sign with the name "Jesse" on it and gave it to me. I hung it on his stall. I was there every day, regardless of the weather, homework, activities, or friends. Life was good, and riding was great.

Eventually, there was another boy. This one had his own horse in the stall next to mine. Mike noticed me long before I noticed him. Being five years my senior, he waited a few weeks before asking me out. Though I was flattered, I declined; I already had a date for the rodeo that evening. He persisted and, without too much of a struggle, he won me over. That's when I discovered that the only thing better than being in love with a horse was being in love with a boy—this boy. I sensed the same qualities in Mike that I felt in Jesse: stability, a sense of adventure, strength, and an abiding love for me.

But there was a problem.

One day Mike and I rode beyond the pasture and into the woods at the back of the property. After dismounting, we threw our arms around each other and began kissing, paying no attention to our horses, tethered loosely a few feet away, contentedly grazing on what little grass was growing under the shady trees. Suddenly, a big brown head pushed its way between us with a snort. Sensing his competition, Jesse shook his mane, rattling his bridle. Mike and I kissed again. Jesse pushed us apart again.

"I don't think he likes me," Mike said.

"Hmmmm. I think you're right," I agreed.

"Well, he's just going to have to get used to me, because I'm not going anywhere but closer to you."

That sounded good to me. "Jesse," I said, "you're just going to have to adjust."

This time, I thought, *I'm going to keep the boy and the horse.*

When Mike proposed, it was with the understanding that we would keep our horses and find a stable close to wherever we lived. His wedding present to me was a beautiful pair of cowboys boots with tiny seed pearls embedded in the tooling. We bought our first house in a new housing development that had recently been a large, open pasture. It still had a barn, where we were able to board the horses, and some acreage, where we could ride them.

When we were expecting our first baby, however, it became more difficult to feed and care for two horses. We had to make another choice.

"Honey, I don't think we can afford to feed the horses and a baby," Mike said.

"Isn't there any way? I just can't imagine selling Jesse."

"We'll try," he said.

We did try, but we soon learned that a baby is even more expensive than a horse, and there really wasn't a choice to make then. We reluctantly decided to sell the animals that had brought us together in the first place.

"We'll have horses again someday, honey," Mike promised.

But, of course, we didn't. Life swept us up with more children, more houses, more jobs, more cities and towns, more life to live and people to love. I kept my saddle and tack for years, but eventually sold them. They took up too much room in the garage. As much as it hurt to release that part of my life, I knew it was time.

Thirty-seven years later, we own 100 acres with a house and a barn, and we have enough money and time to buy horses, ride them, and take care of them. But now I don't want a horse; I don't want to ride anymore. Other loves have captured me, such as grandchildren, writing stories, and lunching with friends. I feel a bit like I've betrayed Jesse, my first love.

Yet, every once in a while, I close my eyes and go back in time . . . to those frosty mornings in the barn, scooping out feed in a plastic bucket, trying to coax Jesse up to the gate so I can saddle him . . . to loping through the pasture, just the two of us, with the wind in my hair . . . to swimming bareback in the lake, my fingers entwined in his coarse mane, laughing and sliding off his back . . . to running the barrels to the loud buzz of the timer, friends cheering and dirt flying. Yes, those days are gone, but Jesse will always be a love affair to remember.

Sally Clark

The Color of Honey and Just as Sweet

"This is a six-year-old palomino quarter horse mare, halter broke only. Two thousand. One thousand. Five hundred. Five hundred dollar bid, who'll give me six? Now seven hundred. Will ya give me eight? I got it!"

I strained to understand the auctioneer's rapid chant, thankful that my friend Pepi had agreed to bid for me. I wouldn't put it past me to make a rookie mistake such as bidding against myself. My companion turned to me with a questioning look in her eyes.

"I'll go as high as a thousand," I said, my jaw clenched and my mind spinning with the fast-paced atmosphere, buzzing with the conversations of hundreds of people. The air was heavy with the odor of hot dogs and anticipation.

"Now nine hundred. How about nine fifty? One thousand! Anyone else in? Sold!"

I stared in disbelief as my first-ever auction purchase exited the small ring that was normally intended for cattle, not horses. Moments later, my friend Judy weaved her way through the crowds to sit next to Pepi and me. Pepi motioned toward the dappled palomino posterior disappearing behind the wide doors.

"Sarah just bought that horse," she announced. Smiling, she looked at me and added, "You'd better go introduce yourself to her."

What was I thinking, buying a horse nearly sight unseen? I knew the dangers of buying at an auction and had been determined to thoroughly review any horse I considered bidding on. I had seen the mare earlier, but I hadn't inspected her. But when that young mare walked into the ring, completely at ease and unfazed by the bustling crowd and fervent shouting, I knew I wanted her. I had promised myself I would buy with my head and not with my heart, and yet there I was, the owner of a horse I knew nothing about.

"Lot 115," the tag pasted to her tail read. I would later joke about naming her Lotis, before settling on calling her Honey. She resembled its color and was just as sweet.

"You'll make a horse out of her," the now-former owner assured me upon encountering me in her stall. I discovered that the fellow had worked with my father twenty years before, but I neglected to garner any of the important information, such as if the mare had been vaccinated or de-wormed. I may not have bid against myself, but I was still acting like a greenhorn, despite having ten years of horse experience.

I bought Honey as a summer project to train and sell, and she proved to be an exceptional purchase. She had the color, temperament, and trainability that everyone desires. After a few weeks of preparatory groundwork, we were ready to saddle up. From then on, I did everything with her—dressage, small jumping courses, Western work, bareback, trail riding, and even riding through the Tim Hortons drive-through to grab a coffee and a carrot muffin! I couldn't believe she had been used only as a broodmare in recent years. There was only one problem: She seemed tender-footed on hard ground. Shoeing her, however, seemed to resolve the problem, or so I thought.

Shortly after I put Honey up for sale in August, a family in a city two hours away looked at her for their young daughter. The petite girl was a little tense while trying her out and toppled off while cantering. Her parents and I rushed over to see if she was all right. Moments later, Honey wandered over, too, and nudged her, as if to say, "Why are you on the ground?" Despite this incident, or perhaps because it demonstrated Honey's kind nature, they took her on trial. They loved her to bits, but when they vetted her, she came up with a slight lameness when trotted on hard ground for an extended period of time. X-rays revealed an anomaly in the navicular bone of one of her hooves. The family wanted to be able to jump her and was told that this could accelerate the problem, which otherwise might not progress any further. Understandably, they chose not to buy her.

I frantically searched for a way to get her back to my city, as neither the family nor I had transportation and the person who had taken her up there was unavailable. I called every professional hauler in the province and didn't get an answer from anyone, except for one person who said he would give me a cut rate because he was coming down anyway. His price was $400. I said to myself, *Heck, I'd ride her back for that much!*

A few days later, another woman from the same city called me and said she had read Honey's updated ad detailing her condition and was interested. I drove up to meet her, and her daughter rode Honey. They adored her and took her home right away, effectively solving the transportation issue. As her mum and I stood talking in the yard, I heard hoof beats approaching and turned around to see the little girl riding Honey saddle-less and bridle-less around the paddock! Her light blonde hair blended with the mare's as she hugged her neck. They were picture-perfect together.

In February, the family got quite the surprise. The weather had been bitterly cold that week, with snowstorms and high winds. The previous weekend had been mild, however, and they had taken the horses to the mountains to ride. Honey had been hesitant to canter, and the reason became evident two days later.

The mother went out to check on the horses that evening to ensure they had plenty of hay and ice-free water. The small herd was standing together, backs to the wind with crystallized snow adorning their rumps. She called to them, but they ignored her; this was odd, as they always came to visit regardless of the weather. Her breath materialized into water vapor as she called to them again, and they reluctantly parted—except for Honey. Carefully making her way through the snow drifts, the woman noticed a shadow below the mare as she approached. She claims that she was never so astonished in her life as when she saw a little colt next to Honey. The herd had been guarding him as best they could from the elements.

Amazingly, Mateo did not suffer any ill effects from his unexpected arrival. He and Honey were immediately transported to a veterinarian, where he was treated for frostbite on his ears and legs. He healed up without incident and was, in fact, so feisty that he had to be pinned to the ground in order to have his bandages changed!

Mateo means "gift of God," and his survival is surely testament to that. It is a fine name, but I maintain that he should have been named Bogo: buy one, get one free.

Sarah Underwood

Heartland

"Horse crazy," my father sighed, half amused, half annoyed, as I galloped from room to room. Before I was old enough to spell my name, my imagination was alive with horses. Tossing manes and pounding hooves lived in my dreams and pranced through the center of my finger paintings. As a four year old, I draped dishtowels from the back of my britches and clip-clopped around the yard, whinnying in my high-pitched voice.

I would climb the cherry tree, where I'd dream about horses stampeding through the orchard. A mighty leap, and I was galloping through the trees, shrieking for joy as the wind whipped my hair. Beyond the orchard, the prairie floor rose up to meet me. Power coursed through me, until . . . what was that sound? I pulled up short to listen.

"Beeekaaaa!" my mother shouted in the distance.

Reality took me by the hand and led me to the dispenser of cookies and hugs. At five, I wasn't prepared to leave the amenities behind.

I wasn't the only one horse-loco. I also made my parents crazy with my incessant begging for a horse. They tried to placate me with half-promises, using words such as "someday" and "maybe." A registered nurse, my mother had seen the results of too many falls. Horses were big, fast, unpredictable. I was fearless. In the end, they had their answer. I was allergic to all things equine.

Meanwhile, my little brother learned what it meant to be a rancher surrounded by horse thieves. His rocking horse was magnetic. I attacked from all angles, forcing him to sleep with his cap gun strapped to his side. My parents joined the posse, repeatedly running me out of town, but to no avail.

I tried bargaining with Santa. He was noncommittal. I coaxed my mother to hire our neighbor to whittle a life-size horse for me. It came again, that quasi-promise: "Maybe someday."

Then life began to change. My father left. He disappeared before I had a chance to say goodbye. Mother never used the word "divorce." She waltzed around it, never getting to the truth. The net result was guilt, confusion, and fear that she might leave us, too.

We moved away, and my mother went to work. A sitter named Louisa took her place. When my mother was around, Louisa smiled a lot. But when we were alone with her, she towered over us and screamed. That's when the nightmares started. Dark horses tearing through my dreams, threatening to carry me away from all I loved. Sometimes I woke crying.

Then one day my mother bought a magic box. It was a television set. Like my imagination, the images on the screen were not confined to the hard edges of reality. Gradually, they seeped into my dreams, bringing solace and safety. Mounted on his white steed, Silver, the Lone Ranger galloped into my dark nights, guarding the borders of my dreams. Louisa didn't like it when I bounced on the sofa shouting, "Hi-O, Silver!" I did it anyway.

For two years I was sustained by my imagination and the sound of my mother's key in the lock. Then, as suddenly as he had disappeared, my father reappeared. There was a quiet ceremony and a new house, where sometimes riders on horseback passed along the undeveloped road, reigniting my hunger for a horse of my own.

In second grade, I got the measles. After a night of fever and delirium, I woke drenched in sweat but coherent. My parents were solicitous. I asked for ice cream and a coloring book of horses. The ice cream part was easy, but they couldn't find a coloring book. Instead they bought a Little Golden Book and drawing paper. I surprised myself with an ability to replicate the horses in the book. After that, I always had a pencil and a pocketful of paper.

Eventually, my penchant for drawing horses got me into trouble. With grandiose plans to upgrade Grandma's neighborhood, I used a bottle of black shoe polish to paint an oversized work of the Black Stallion, blindfolded and rearing, on the sidewalk in front of her house. By then, I was nearly twelve. I was genuinely shocked to learn how little my grandmother appreciated my contribution to the art world. She scolded me severely, calling my work "thoughtless graffiti." What she never knew was how close I'd come to painting my mural on the side of her white stucco house.

After the measles, it took my father less than a year to lose his job. He became distant and unapproachable. The house went up for sale. On the day his final paycheck came, he startled me by asking me to take a walk with him. We ended up in a little shop a mile or so from home. He looked around, then pointed to a set of three glass horses. "You like those?" he asked.

I nodded, my heart pounding.

"I'll take those for my little girl."

I was stunned. I carried them home in a brown paper bag clutched to my chest. For years they were my most prized possession, until a fire swept through our home, destroying everything we owned.

After my father lost his job, we moved to Grandma's. Mother went to work again. My father drank. That summer I met Sarah, who lived around the corner. At last I'd found a kindred spirit. Sarah had a wide imagination. She understood my passion for horses. Hula hoops became harnesses as we pulled each other around the yard. We spent our money on plastic horses and built corrals of twigs beneath the elms. We fell in love with the Cisco Kid and even shook his hand one time, while coveting his horse. We trekked around local stables, soaking in the smell of horses and hay, until a man in dusty blue jeans pointed to the sign that said "private property" and invited us to leave.

At work that year, my mother met a nurse named Ella. When the talk turned to my keen interest in horses, Ella was impressed. Though she was at least a decade older than my mother, she was an active horsewoman. Miraculously, my mother asked if Ella would allow me to ride with her sometime. She promised she'd stop by. I nearly died of joy when my mother told me. Weeks went by. Though I pestered my mother mercilessly, Ella postponed her promise repeatedly. Then one glorious afternoon she showed up, decked out in black and silver from head to toe. I was ready to take the reins and ride like the wind. Instead, I sat in back as Ella walked us clippidy-clop, clippidy-clop down the paved street. It was a short, stiff ride that left me starving for more.

Days later, after I'd driven my mother nearly mad begging for another ride, she sat me down with an emphatic "No!" She took a breath and then explained. There was a reason, she said, for Ella's reticence, a reason for the short, stiff ride. It wouldn't be fair or kind to ask again. Earlier in life, she said, Ella had been blessed with a daughter who was as much in love with horses as I was. As they rode together and cared for their animals, a secure bond formed between them. That bond was tragically shattered when a low-hanging branch caught her young daughter off-guard and swept her to her death. The prospect of riding with another child rekindled Ella's fear and called forth remnants of her pain leftover from that day. I didn't ask again. If my mother meant to impress me that day with the risks a large and powerful animal could impose, she succeeded. My illusions were becoming painfully tight.

Grandma was chafing to have her space again. This time, we moved to a run-down apartment above the

Chevrolet garage on Main Street. My father spiraled deeper into drinking and despondency. In the summer of my eleventh year, a raging fire swept through our building, leaving us with only our lives and, in my case, half a pair of pajamas. Childhood was ending abruptly. Before I could say goodbye, it was gone. Sixth grade, the turmoil of adolescence, high school teachers who dismissed my idealized drawings—dreaming came harder with all that. As the years rolled on, the cares and adversities of life pressed out the remembrance of childhood dreams, and the drumbeat of horses' hooves receded into forgotten places.

Then one day I looked in the mirror and saw a fifty-seven-year-old woman about to board a plane to Kentucky. I looked at the lines around my eyes, the gray hair at my temples, and wondered where life had gone. The answer wasn't hard to find. I'd raised six children, now all grown. The youngest, though, remained a child, shuffling daily through the cluttering world of autism. I seldom spent a day away from him. But now I watched the ground recede, felt the miles disappear beneath me. I was going to spend Easter with my children and grandchildren who lived a thousand miles away.

The weekend was warm with hugs, jelly bird eggs, a beautiful drenching rainstorm that brought out the resident rabbit, and the joyous songs of Easter.

Pink dogwoods exploded like candied popcorn throughout Louisville, which was winding up to the Kentucky Derby.

The day before I left for home, we piled into the van and drove out of town to explore Old Friends, a retirement and rescue farm for Thoroughbreds. The farm was quiet, Kentucky green, punctuated with trees. Large enclosures sprawled beneath the afternoon sky. We followed our guide as she recited the accomplishments of each horse. A gentle breeze tucked my hair back. I walked leisurely, speaking quietly as we moved along: "Hi there, big guy." "Hello, pretty girl." But the connection as I had once known it was gone . . . until Popcorn.

Used in the race-start scenes of the movie *Seabiscuit*, Popcorn Deelites responded to our guide's signal by galloping from the far corner of a wide enclosure. Coming to a halt, he put his nose over the fence. Instinctively, I put my hand out to him. His baby-soft muzzle nestled into my palm, feeling for tidbits. I felt the warm breath of his nostrils on my wrist. In an instant, the years fell away, the dreams of my childhood opened around me in an array of sparkling colors, as present as if they had never been lost. I leaned in, ran my hand along his nose. I was a child again, my joy washing over me like a warm wind. I tried to memorize every detail of that moment as our group began to drift away. Then, in a heartbeat, he was gone, galloping back into the sunlit field. With an edge of pleading in my voice, I asked the guide to call him back.

"Popcorn!"

He didn't respond. I stood transfixed, listening to the sound of pounding hooves recede into the distance, every instinct inside me screaming to recall him. Instead, I heard myself whisper, "Goodbye. Goodbye, Popcorn." He was gone. It wasn't meant for him to stay, but he had given me a gift I would never forget—a remembrance of my childhood and a chance to say goodbye. In a quiet moment of connection, he had drawn a golden bridge between the present and the past and allowed me to pass over it.

I walked slowly, treasuring the moment—one that would stay with me long after the pink dogwoods of Kentucky disappeared beneath the clouds. My father was right. Whether you called it craziness or something else, I was born connected to the echoing beat of horses running through the heartland of my soul.

Rebekah Schow

My Trail Guardian

When I was sixty-four, a year after I'd retired from my school administration job, my husband, Jim, and I hooked the horse trailer to our pickup truck and went shopping for a trail horse for me, answering ads in the Phoenix, Arizona, newspaper. I had been riding a young horse we'd kept after Jim decided to quit the horse-breeding business. He had been raising show horses since his retirement.

We had never before shopped for a horse that way. We had always either bought our horses from breeders or trainers we knew or raised them ourselves. Jim and I were amazed at the plethora of spoiled horses—some too old, many with uncared-for hooves, some who wouldn't load in the trailer, most over-priced, and all a far cry from what the ads had described. Ready to give up by late afternoon, we decided to look at one more horse.

The advertised horse was Dolly, a nine-year-old, dark buckskin quarter horse mare with black mane and tail and four black stockings. Jim rode Dolly, and she seemed calm and an easy rider. I rode Dolly. She reined well and changed gaits easily on cue. We bought her. The ad said she was "papered."

The seller gave us papers indicating Dolly was a registered quarter horse as advertised. The owner signed the transfer papers, but confessed she would have to contact the other owner, who was out of town. If he ever came back to town, no one contacted us. Without his signature, Dolly could not be registered, but by the time all that mailing had taken place, it didn't matter to me. I had already bonded more than I had with any other horse.

I had been riding all my life, but I didn't have the born-in balance of my husband and some riders with whom we trail-rode. It didn't take much of a buck for me to fall off. Dolly never bucked. She seemed to enjoy being a lady's trail horse, as though she felt a responsibility to see to my welfare. I couldn't make her do something if she thought it was dangerous. I couldn't get lost riding her. She always knew her way back to the trailer or the barn.

Dolly proved this to skeptics one day on a camp-and-ride with the Payson, Arizona, Saddle Club. We were heading back to camp after a day's ride. When we came to a fork in the road, the trail boss (who just happened to be my husband that day) decided to take a shortcut (as he claimed). Dolly would have no part of it. She insisted the fork he wanted to take wasn't going to get us back to camp. I pulled a Forest Service map of the area from my saddlebag and pointed out to the trail boss that the trail he selected didn't appear to go all the way to our campsite. By then I had learned to trust Dolly's sense of direction.

"I think I'll go with Dolly," I said. "I'm tired. Anyone else want to go with me?"

That was really poor trail manners, because the trail boss was the head honcho and the riders were supposed to go where he led them, but I was fatigued. Dolly and I took off. No one came with me. My husband knew I was safe with Dolly. I held the reins loosely, and soon she lengthened into a running walk.

I was enjoying a glass of wine and hors d'oeuvres around the campfire, while the camp tenders worried about the missing riders. An hour later, they straggled in, my husband looking sheepish. Turns out the trail they took just led to the top of a mesa overlooking the camp with no trail down. They had to backtrack to the fork where I had parted from them.

Dolly had a sense of humor and an adventurous spirit. Jim and I were staying near Pagosa Springs, Colorado, and planning a three-day trip into the Weminuche Wilderness. We decided to make an overnighter to Sand Creek to see how well we could pack enough gear on our two horses for camping out without using a packhorse.

When we reached the Sand Creek camp spot, we just barely got our two-person tent up and our belongings under shelter when it rained. We crawled into the tent to wait out the storm, leaving the horses hobbled outside.

Over the sound of the rain pelting our tent, I heard a *clop, clop, clop.* I looked out the screened tent window. Dolly was jumping, hobbled, up the trail.

"Dolly, come back here!" I yelled.

She glanced back, hesitated, and then took a couple more jumps. Jim's gelding, Hornet, was trying to follow her.

I crawled out of the tent and stood up in the rain, which was beginning to slack off. "Dolly! You better come back here!" I yelled again.

She looked back at me, with what I swear was a grin, then turned and clopped back to where Hornet stood. I reached inside the tent and retrieved a handful of sweet feed and gave it to her.

On our way back over the Sand Creek Trail the next morning, Jim was in the lead, and Dolly and I were close behind. The trail dropped off to my left down to the creek in its canyon, and the mountain rose up to my right. Suddenly Dolly snorted and took off at a lope, going around Jim and Hornet on the slope until it leveled out through the forest. I was finally able to pull her up and wait for Jim.

"What brought that on?" I wondered aloud. "Did she look down at the drop to the creek and get scared? She never has before."

"No," he said. "She smelled or saw the black bear that came up out of the canyon right behind you."

The bear was no longer anywhere we could see, and Dolly was calm.

In 1982, we sold our place in Phoenix and moved to Camp Verde, Arizona, where Jim realized his dream of owning his own irrigated pasture. We bought a two-acre ranchette with a house and a concrete ditch carrying water from the Verde River for irrigation.

We were on another camp-and-ride with the Payson Saddle Club, this time on the Mogollon Rim. We were riding in a tall ponderosa pine forest on a trail that made a steep climb down to and across a canyon and back up. The trail was wide enough for only one horse, with a sheer drop-off to our left and a steep slope rising up from the other side. It is spectacularly rugged country, and the altitude is about 7,000 feet.

About an hour from camp, I fainted in the saddle. When I regained consciousness, Dolly was standing very still, crowding the up-slope rather than the drop, while I was hanging with my head down to her belly, my right foot out of the stirrup. She did not take another step until I was upright in the saddle, both feet firmly in the stirrups.

By then my husband had heard the commotion among the riders near me, but he couldn't turn around his horse and get back to me on the narrow trail. I could think of no physical reason that might have caused me to faint. Never before in my life had I fainted.

After the shock wore off, I patted Dolly's neck. How fortunate that Dolly had stayed calm and not spooked when I almost went out of the saddle. If she had shied or bucked, I would have tumbled down the steep incline a thousand feet, unless a tree broke my fall. I passed the word to Jim that I would be all right; Dolly would take care of me.

The next day I went out again on the scheduled ride. The first part of the trail was through the forest on level ground and easy riding. I fainted again.

Again Dolly stopped, but this time when I righted myself, Dolly turned and started back to camp. I didn't object. She knew what was good for me. The drag rider, as is customary, went with me to make sure I made it back.

I fainted again in camp, and the camp tenders around me said it looked like I might be having a seizure. I didn't ride again on that trip. On my return home I went immediately to see my doctor, a general practitioner. After having me tested for seizure activity and other problems, he referred me to an internist.

The internist quickly diagnosed a heart condition known as PAT, *paroxysmal arrhythmia tachycardia*, an irregular heart beat. At times my heart's irregularity caused me to faint. Medication took care of the problem. At the time, in 1986, I was seventy years old and Dolly was fifteen.

I rode Dolly until my husband had a stroke in 1992 and could no longer ride. We sold our home in Camp Verde, and I gave Dolly to a friend who wanted a gentle horse for his little girl to ride. Though I never rode again, I took comfort in knowing that Dolly would guard over her new charge as diligently as she had me.

Jean R. Clark

Four Legs, Two Wheels, One Wish

Trail riding and campouts, dashing around barrels and poles in play days, feeding and grooming: Martha devoted all her spare time to her beloved horses. Poncho, the gray American quarter horse gelding, excelled in gymkhana events, while Chico, a young bay-grade gelding, was Martha's favorite trail mount. She loved riding; it gave her a sense of freedom. The horses also gave Martha, a single woman living alone, companionship and purpose.

A rainy Oregon winter was well underway, curtailing Martha's outdoor activities. Though she still loaded up the two geldings and hauled them to the local fairgrounds for monthly saddle club rides in the covered arena, she missed the frequent trail rides. Being outdoors with her horses not only gave Martha pleasure, it also helped to relieve her stress.

Recently, Martha's job had become quite stressful. At fifty-eight, Martha hadn't grown up with computers like the younger generation. Mastering spreadsheets had been a great accomplishment for her, but now she also had new data entry tracking systems to learn. To make matters worse, other employees had been laid off, so more of the workload came Martha's way. On top of that, she'd caught a nasty cold that had been lingering for weeks.

After a long day at work followed by an hour-long commute home, Martha looked forward to Poncho and Chico nuzzling her over their stall doors. Martha's horses were always there when she needed a shoulder to lean on or someone to hug.

The long, gray winter finally gave way to spring with its longer daylight hours and better weather. But what Martha thought was a minor cold soon proved to be a nasty flu, and she just wasn't up to riding or even play days. She stayed home from work an entire week, trying to nurse herself back to health. Despite Martha's fatigue and malaise, she faithfully trudged to the barn morning and night to care for her horses. They were the bright spot in her day.

One Thursday evening in April, Martha was feeling well enough to host a committee meeting of her riding club in her home. The small group of friends discussed plans for an upcoming play day, related how their horses were shedding buckets of hair, and talked about life in general. By 9:30, everyone had left. Martha put the coffee cups in the dishwasher and the leftover snacks in the cupboard. She turned in shortly thereafter and fell fast asleep.

When Martha awoke the next morning, she noticed a slight tingling in her right leg. Thinking it must have been "asleep," she got up and walked to the bathroom. After changing clothes and heading for the barn, the tingling hadn't disappeared and had actually increased. She filled the geldings' water buckets. The strange sensation was progressing to the other leg. She was getting quite concerned, so she tossed each horse several flakes of hay, wondering if she'd be able to make it back to the barn for evening chores. Walking back to the house proved difficult. The tingling gave way to numbness. Her legs were failing. By the time Martha reached her kitchen door, she dropped to her knees. Thankfully, the phone was just inside the door. Trembling, she dialed 9-1-1.

The paramedics placed Martha on a stretcher and zoomed to the hospital. Tests were performed; doctors conferred. The diagnosis: Guillain-Barré syndrome, a neurological disorder that often causes muscle weakness and paralysis.

Martha's legs were completely paralyzed. How could this be? While the cause was unclear, doctors suspected that her immune system might have been depressed due to stress and illness during the preceding months. They explained that in most cases, patients make a satisfactory recovery and eventually regain use of their legs.

Martha was released to a rehabilitation center a week later. Determined to regain her health, Martha carefully followed the therapist's instructions. Her initial progress was amazing, and the medical staff all thought she was well on her way to recovery. However, Martha's progress began to slow. Other therapists were called in. After reviewing her case, they were still very hopeful. Setbacks can happen, they explained, but progress usually continues. In Martha's case, it did not.

After six months of intensive physical therapy in the rehabilitation center, Martha was outfitted with a wheelchair and released to return home. Her brother, Adam, had shared the care of Poncho and Chico with several neighbors.

When Adam drove Martha home, she asked to go straight to the barn to see the geldings. The wheelchair bumped and jostled over the narrow gravel path. Once inside the barn, the chair rolled easily down the aisle. At the first door, Poncho stretched his long neck over the stall door to sniff the back of the chair and then the woman's thick gray hair. Recognizing his owner, he whickered softly and nuzzled Martha's cheek. Tears came to her eyes as she patted his glossy neck. Soon Chico welcomed Martha with a loud whinny.

Adam and the neighbors made wheelchair accommodations to Martha's home and surroundings, including paving the path to the barn. She could now get herself to the barn to see the geldings. Their presence always brightened her spirits, but she longed to ride again. As days came and went, hope of walking or riding dimmed. The geldings were too big and risky for her to even lead them.

One day Martha's old friend Sarah was thumbing through an equestrian magazine when an article about miniature horses caught her eye. It mentioned that some minis are used as therapy and companion animals. *That's the answer!* Sarah thought. *If Martha had a mini, she could safely groom and lead it.* So Sarah began searching for the right miniature for Martha.

A few weeks later, Sarah went to visit Martha. As her dear friend lamented about not being able do anything with her geldings, Sarah knew she'd done the right thing. Soon they heard a pickup truck rumbling up the driveway. Martha wondered who it could possibly be. Sarah pushed the wheelchair out into the yard just as the pickup slowed to a stop. Martha was surprised to see the truck was pulling a horse trailer.

The driver, Jim, jumped out. The tall man in jeans and a tan canvas jacket strode to the trailer door and swung it open to reveal a tiny pinto horse. He untied the rope and led the horse to the end of the trailer. The horse glanced down and leaped to the ground. Jim led him over to Martha. In her seated position, the horse was no taller than her waist. She threw her arms around the black and white neck. It was the first time in months she'd been able to hug a horse. Tears of joy streamed down all of their faces, even Jim's.

The little pinto, Sarah explained, was named Toby. He'd belonged to a family whose kids had grown up and lost interest in him. When the parents heard about Martha, they knew she could offer Toby the perfect home

Then Jim went to the back of the pickup and lifted out a small suitcase followed by a miniature easy entry cart. He opened the suitcase to display a tiny black harness with brass fittings. Toby was broke to drive! His former owners assured Sarah that he was very safe and dependable in the cart.

During the coming week, Martha went to the barn several times a day to get acquainted with Toby and groom him. He would lay his little head on her lap while she brushed his fluffy mane. They were quickly developing a special relationship. He rallied her spirits, and her whole outlook on life improved.

Lying in bed one night, unable to move her legs without the help of her hands, Martha realized it was time to let the geldings go. They were much too nice of saddle horses to stand around doing nothing. Caring for them from a wheelchair had become a burden, and their sheer size posed a safety risk for her. Martha asked Sarah to find them good homes, but only on lease, just in case.

The following weekend Sarah hitched up Martha's trailer and loaded Toby, the cart, and harness. Off they went to the indoor arena at the fairgrounds. Toby was unflappable as Sarah harnessed and hitched him. She warmed him up for a few circles and then stopped next to the wheelchair. She helped Martha maneuver from the chair to the seat of the cart. Once Martha was settled in, Sarah handed her the driving lines. Toby responded readily to her subtle cues. He was relaxed as he first walked and then trotted around the arena. Soon Martha had him trotting a figure eight. Martha had regained her equestrian freedom! And with her newfound independence, the gloom that had shadowed her for all those months finally began to lift.

Traci Durrell-Khalife

Run Like the Wind

The horse galloped along the levee on that early Mississippi summer evening, turned suddenly, gathered his hind legs under him, and with muscles quivering, leapt into the air. The forward thrust propelled him and his thirteen-year-old female rider into the water of the 100-acre lake. They went deep, then deeper still, cocooned in warm, murky water. Powerful strokes of the horse's legs brought them to the surface in what seemed an eternity to the young rider. She had no choice but to hang on. She couldn't swim.

When their heads broke the surface of the water, the girl gasped for breath and then coughed the foul, fishy lake water from her lungs. The horse, never faltering, swam as surely and faithfully as an Olympic athlete. The young teen held on, her cramped fingers locked on the saddle horn in a death grip. She floated on top of the water beside the horse and felt every movement of his muscles as he swam unerringly to the far shore, pulling her along with him.

Buck was a good horse. At age seven, he was in his prime. His half Thoroughbred, half quarter horse breeding gave him long legs, a muscular body, and the stamina and "let's go" attitude of a race horse. His slick bay coat glistened like fire, and his flowing ebony mane and tail sparkled with highlights of blue in the sun's rays. Buck loved his new young owner and would do anything she asked of him—even jump into a lake at the risk of his own life.

When Buck got to shallow water, I slipped easily back into the saddle. He waded up on shore, and I slid off him. I removed his saddle, blanket, and bridle and threw them on a tree limb to dry. I removed my own clothes and hung them on another bush to dry. Buck lay down and rolled, as all wet horses will do. Then he wandered off to graze tender green shoots of grass while I found a bed of leaves and took a nap in the sun.

I woke up and lay there very still as I watched a doe and her fawn drinking from the lake. Beavers were busy working on their dam at the spillway, and an alligator was lazily swimming on the surface at the other end of the lake. Honey bees were buzzing and flitting from one wild flower to the next. Birds chirped their cheerful songs while an old white crane stood in the shallows with a watchful eye for his supper. Green striped bass leapt far up in the air after flies that floated on the smooth, glasslike surface of the water. The sun was setting in a brilliant orb of crimson over the top of the hill.

Sunset! Oh no! I had chores to do!

I had my clothes on and Buck saddled-ride within minutes. All the while, I was estimating how long it would take us to get home, and I didn't like the odds. "Buck, ole boy, run like the wind! If I have to go behind that woodshed for being late, you're going right along with me." Buck did run like the wind. He didn't want to go behind the woodshed either.

I had been riding farm horses since I was two years old, but I wanted one of my own. On my thirteenth birthday, in April, 1970, my father presented me with Buck. He was everything I'd hoped for and then some. I loved him with all the passion of a young girl, and he, in turn, loved me. Together, we had many adventures—some of which, in hindsight, I now wonder how we survived. God must watch over young fools.

I grew up in a different world than the one we live in today. In our small, rural, Mississippi town in

the late sixties and early seventies, there was com-
paratively little crime, and most kids were free to
come and go pretty much as we pleased, as long as
we'd done our chores. With Buck, I could go wherever I wanted. And go we did. Because he could
cover 50 miles a day with ease, my life opened up to
one with few boundaries.

There were so many places to go and so much to
see. Several government lakes were scattered around
the countryside, and Buck and I missed very few of
them. Buck never refused to jump into anything I
asked him to, and a cool dip in the water after riding
for hours on a hot summer day was the perfect way
to cool us off. Though I couldn't swim, I never felt a
twinge of fear, because I trusted that horse to get me
to safety, and he always did.

Neighboring towns were now within my reach.
A twenty-mile ride and a few good horse races always
netted me candy bars or Cokes. Buck, with his Thoroughbred blood, ran like the wind, and he became
known throughout the area as a race-winning horse.
He was the subject of many conversations in all
those little towns. "Buck's in town," I'd overhear as
I rode in. People would come out and ask me who
I had raced and by how many lengths I had beat
them. This was heady stuff for a thirteen-year-old.
No one knew how old I was, and because I was off

alone on this horse in their town, they assumed I was nearly grown. They treated me with the respect usually allotted to an adult. Life couldn't have been sweeter.

The problem with growing up in that era was that everybody in town knew everybody else in town. They had known me since I was born or since I'd made my first appearance at church. I knew the names of all the kids and all their parents and grand-parents, and they all knew mine. This contributed to my safety on some of my escapades, but it also hampered my being able to go to neighboring towns every Saturday. I was free to go anywhere in the town where I lived, but I knew if I got caught in another town my daddy would take me behind the woodshed. You did not want to go behind the wood-shed with Daddy for any reason. It always resulted in standing up for your meals for three days.

My days of going to other towns to race Buck against the neighboring horses came to an abrupt end with a conversation I overheard between my daddy and a man who had come to buy a hunting dog. The stranger was telling him about a young woman on a fast bay horse who won every race. This got Daddy's attention, not because he for one minute thought it might be me, but because he was always interested in a fast horse. The good Lord was on my side in that the stranger had not seen me race and had only heard the stories in the neighboring towns where no one knew my name.

Then and there, Buck and I retired from horse racing in other towns. We stuck to our local haunts after that. Never mind that we were sometimes off on back roads, miles away from any human eye, or that we were jumping off levees into lakes nestled in forests you could get to only by following a deer path. To this day, my parents have no clue that I was doing any of that, and I will never tell them. My daddy still has that woodshed.

Wanda West

A Forelock to Lean On

My story is not of awe-inspiring endeavors, amazing accomplishments, or miraculous events. While my life with horses these past fifteen years has included all that, it is not the most important part of my relationship with horses.

I started riding when I was five years old, and since then, not a day has gone by that I haven't spent with or daydreaming about horses. I took lessons at a well-known hunter/jumper barn and progressed quickly. Though my parents could not afford to buy me a horse, just being at the barn filled me with joy and happiness. As I grew older, I was able to lease a pony and then a horse. While all the other girls my age at the barn went to horse shows every weekend, I was overjoyed with the two horse shows I got to do a year. More than anything, I just loved my horse.

At thirteen, I had outgrown my leased horse, and my parents decided it was the right time to buy one for me, with the promise that someday I'd pay them back (which I did a few years later). Knowing my trainer would be unable to find a horse in our low price range, I set off on a quest to find my perfect equine partner. I rode two horses with no success before I found the horse of my dreams. The minute I walked into the dimly lit stall and saw him—a small gelding, barely 16.2 hands high, with a dull bay coat, a dark black mane and tail, and Warmblood-sized ears that could give a donkey a run for their money—I knew he was the one. Talk about love at first sight! There was something different about this horse. He didn't greet me or make a fuss. He simply stood there, glancing at me long enough to get across the message, *Who do you think you are?*

When the breeders turned him out in the arena, a spark lit his eyes. He galloped around the ring as if he'd sprouted heavenly wings upon his back. He approached and cleared fences as if they were his toys. Then I rode him for the first time. It was amazing. His large, floating gates swept across the ground, and his jump was strong and smooth. After a vet exam, a sales contract, and a signed check, he was mine.

I quickly learned that Dino was not a horse that loved to be scratched and rubbed or messed with.

Although he grew to love me over the next five years and turned out to be very sweet, he never went out of his way to be with me. I trained him into a lovely dressage horse and jumper. In that respect, he was everything I wanted: competitive, passionate, free-spirited (if a little too opinionated sometimes), and full of life and vigor. Many days, I sat in the corner of Dino's stall and just watched him, sometimes wishing that he were a little more affectionate or even a little more interested in me. As I watched him, he might sniff me for a moment, but then he'd return to munching on his hay or peering out the window into the crystal blue sky.

My family grew to love Dino, too, especially my father. Although Dad was by no means a horse person, he became very attached to my little gelding. He fed him countless carrots and brushed him until he shined like the sun. My father was never prouder than when he watched his "little girl" riding the "big" Warmblood. Some of my favorite memories are of my dad out at the barn watching me ride and spoiling my horse. Dino was usually a pretty high-strung horse, but he always knew to walk quietly and carefully when my dad wanted to lead him down the aisle or brush his face or when a small child was placed upon his back. He seemed to always know what to do when it counted.

I vowed never to sell Dino, and he even came with me when I went to college in Florida. During my second year away at school, my father was diagnosed with lung cancer. The doctors initially gave him six months to live, but after hearing the cancer wasn't responding to treatment, we knew we didn't have much time. I was as brave as I could be, never crying, never letting myself crumble. But no matter how long a person tries to be strong, losing a loved one will break you like you've never been broken before.

My breaking point came on a sunny day in October. As I entered the barn where my horse was boarded, a cool breeze swept my blonde hair across my weary face. Nobody was around, and I was glad of that. I took a folding chair and slowly walked into my horse's stall, shutting the door behind me. I sat down on the chair in the corner of his stall, as I'd done so many times before. Suddenly, the wall of strength that had been holding me together gave way, and the pain I had kept inside released as if from a broken dam. I buried my head in my hands and wept with the grief of knowing my father's life would soon be over. In the depths of my despair, I felt a velvet nose nuzzling my hair and puffs of warm breath against my scalp. It was my little gelding—the fiercely independent Warmblood who was usually too absorbed in his own plan to come and be affectionate with me, who usually tossed his head in defiance when I tried to hug and hold him. I raised my head, looking up through my tears into his bright bay face. He stepped closer and lowered his nose into my lap, placing his head by my chest. I wrapped my arms around his wide head and leaned my face onto his forehead. It was the comfort I needed, just like the comfort my father used to give me when he scooped me up into his arms and held me. The horse who rarely held still, who was always on the move looking for adventure, stood perfectly still for more than twenty minutes while I cried into his black forelock.

A true friend stands with you in times of joy and sorrow and in times of celebration and tribulation. When I needed Dino's friendship most, when it felt like my world was coming to an end, my gelding stepped forward and gave me friendship's greatest gifts: his consolation and affection. So this story is not about the excitement of horse shows and championships, or the glory of ribbons and trophies, or the satisfaction of achieving career-altering goals, or even the importance of learning new things. It is about the blessing of love. Pure and simple.

Lauren C. Esping

Riding Blind

When I was a kid, I lived for horseback riding. But money was tight, so I got one precious hour in the saddle a week. Money got even tighter when I was sixteen and my parents divorced. They made it painfully clear that after my high school graduation, there would be no more riding lessons because of college costs. With the clock ticking oppressively on, I was determined to enjoy every minute I could get in the saddle.

So it was one beautiful, spring Saturday morning—my one and only chance to ride that week. *Oh, this is gonna be sweet,* I thought as I approached the bright bay, Timmy. As he waited patiently for me to mount, he stared at the jumps in the next field. Timmy was an elderly Tennessee walker/Arabian mix still draped in muscle. In his youth, he was a bold fox hunter, and he still hauled on the bit whenever he saw a jump. I pushed my glasses up my sweaty nose and hoisted myself into the saddle as lightly as I could.

The lesson began as usual. There were only two of us, me on Timmy and another girl on Joey, a retired racehorse. We walked, trotted, and cantered around a homemade ring next to a six-stall stable and a huge, tree-studded field of jumps and runs. Old Mr. McVeigh owned the land and the horses. He supplemented his pension by renting out his horses to crazy girls like me.

As usual, Timmy showed every day of his age in the ring, shuffling and sighing in boredom. He saved all of his brilliance for the jumps.

Mr. McVeigh suggested we trot without stirrups, which is one of the very few activities I don't miss about riding. I'm convinced this was invented by the Marquis de Sade. Bang, bang, bang went my behind to the beat of Timmy's clunky trot. This time, Timmy reached his limit before I did. He bolted.

I grimly hung on, but I couldn't stop from sailing off of the slippery slope of Timmy's right shoulder. I slammed onto the ground, flat on my back. Little did I know that my glasses had flown off. I figured that blurred vision was normal after getting the wind knocked out of you. I'd done what my dad would call "Rena's flying dismount." Luckily, it was Mom's weekend with me, and she was chatting to the other rider's mother, oblivious to the lesson. I was nearly blind without my glasses because I have extreme near-sightedness and virtually no depth perception.

"You okay?" Mr. McVeigh asked—at least, I think it was Mr. McVeigh. All I could see was a big blur bending over me.

"What did I do wrong?" I gasped.

"You braced yourself before landing. That's what you did wrong. When you know you're gonna fall, just relax and flop off. Me, I'm so relaxed when I fall, I read a magazine on the way down."

I sat up and said, "Uh . . . everything's fuzzy."

"Well, your glasses are broken. Here, I picked up the pieces for you."

No! Not on a riding day with perfect weather and Timmy dying to jump! I was glad to realize I wasn't hurt, but now my crummy eyes would screw up this chance. As soon as Mom found out, I'd be yanked out of there and hauled to the optician's. Life stinks.

"You ready to get back on?" Mr. McVeigh asked kindly, helping me to my feet with one hand and holding onto Timmy's reins with the other.

"I'm fine now," I lied, staring at the blurry patch of smeared shapes that smelled like Timmy. "I can ride without my glasses."

"Atta girl!" Mr. McVeigh said. "Let me give you a leg up."

Somehow my hands connected with the reins. Mr. McVeigh only saw me one hour a week. He didn't have a clue as to how blind I was! But he was going to let me ride his Timmy, and that's all that mattered to me. I must've been grinning like an idiot.

I settled into the saddle and tried to move into Timmy's walk, which suddenly seemed smoother than usual, into the swirling kaleidoscope of cloudy colors that is the natural way I see the world. I couldn't even see the fence! I assumed the big dark blur was Joey carrying the other girl and that the little blur was Mr. McVeigh, but I couldn't be sure.

I wondered how long I could keep this charade going. I also wondered how long I would continue living. That fall hurt! At least I could put my stirrups back on.

I finally managed to merge into Timmy's walk, soothing and energizing me simultaneously. I let my weight sink down into my heels and seat bones, and I breathed deeply.

"Posting trot!" Mr. McVeigh called.

Timmy shifted gears without the usual lurch. He didn't plod now, but rather, stretched out in his smooth field trot. We rippled through the blurry air.

I didn't think; I just rode. I ignored what my eyes were telling me and just felt my way along with Timmy. And we never collided into Joey, which was an extra bonus. I wasn't even being yelled at about cutting corners. Timmy made me look good all on his own.

Then it was time to leave the ring for the field. Timmy seemed to expand all around me, but I still felt a part of him. Joey went first, and darn it, if we didn't pop over three- and four-foot post and rails as if they were cavelleti poles. I just let Timmy do it and stayed out of his way. I could feel his muscles bunch up, and that clued me for his leap. We never had a problem.

That exercise ended the supervised lesson. Then it was free time, when Mr. McVeigh would let us goof around for a few turns about the field, then come back to him at a walk, so he could ready the horses for the next pair of students.

Joey and Timmy were always competitive. Each *had* to be in front of the other. Even blind, I knew Timmy's eyes sparkled by the way he pulled.

Joey's rider called, "Race you!" and thundered off.

I don't remember who won. But galloping on Timmy blind is a sensation I've never found a comparison to in all the years since. I hope that heaven winds up being that same race, blind on Timmy, bent over him and feeling the tree branches scratch as we sailed by.

Mom was not exactly thrilled when she discovered I'd ridden without my glasses. But she had the grace not to throttle Mr. McVeigh and even verbally thanked Timmy for bringing me back to her.

I reluctantly dismounted, then hugged Timmy. But he ignored me, his head once again turned to stare at the jumps. But I was close enough to see his face clearly when he finally glanced at me as if to say, "Just you wait until you get your new glasses. The ride will be mighty different then!"

Rena Sherwood

Trinity

A blast of damp April air hits me in the face when I open the door to a bleak afternoon. "Not too promising out here," I say to Maxx, my German shepherd, as I pull the collar of my coat tight around my neck and turtle my head deep inside. Pausing on the deck, I study the gray-bellied stratus clouds mottling the sky, bumping along on the sporadic gusts of a northwest wind. The faint sun has poked holes in the dingy snow banks that ring our yard. The air smells faintly of dirt, not the fresh smell of newly turned soil being readied for a crop but, rather, like the inside of a vacuum cleaner bag. There is a sense of nature holding its breath, waiting for the first cold rains of spring to wash away all the grit and refresh the Earth.

Yup, a day without promise, I think.

Maxx takes all four stairs in one leap, interrupting my gloomy thoughts, and I bound after him. I hopscotch around mud puddles on the way to my three-quarter-ton pickup, scanning the corral for Daisy, our dainty, dappled pony, who is large with foal and due any day. The absence of a whinny escapes me as I open the back of the topper for Maxx to hop in and circle around to the cab. Daisy and I are both preoccupied, she with doing pony-ish things, I with double-checking my errand list—pick up kids, groceries, grain, shots for the foal. . . .

The foal.

I again scan for Daisy and spot her diligently walking laps in the corral. She stops, increases the manure piles by one, and walks on. Nothing out of the ordinary catches my eye, so I return to my list. A few moments later I feel compelled to check on Daisy again and am surprised to see her making a second manure pile. *Hmm . . . it's too soon, but is she in labor?*

I watch Daisy move off. . . . Yes, there she goes again, back humped up, tail flagging. My plans have just changed. The errand list is forgotten; I am on full midwife alert.

Maxx hits the ground running when I let him out of the truck. His tongue lolls around the big doggy grin on his face that mirrors the grin on mine.

We both make a brisk line for the corral, jumping over snow banks.

Daisy's confusion about the arrival of her first foal is evident, but I can barely contain my excitement. I follow her, carefully sidestepping muck, and notice many worry wrinkles above her eyes.

"Daisy," I call softly, grabbing a lead rope off the post.

She turns to me, ears pricked, eyes questioning, and then walks to meet me. She pushes her soft muzzle under my arm and hides her eyes in the folds of my coat. I stroke her neck and feel her muscles tense and quiver under my palm.

"Poor little mama," I reassure her, as birds chirp warnings from bare branches and the sun desperately tries to break free of the clouds. I snap the lead to Daisy's halter and guide her carefully to the gate.

Maxx yips and dances in agitation, while Daisy and I stop as she endures one more contraction. Soft breezes play with her flaxen mane and tail, the delicate silver strands flashing in the sunlight. When we reach the barn, I turn Daisy loose inside the deeply bedded foaling stall and shut the door. Sensing my excitement, Maxx whines as he follows me into the storeroom. Quickly, I grab towels, iodine, an aspirator, a pail of hot soapy water, and a very large, disposable obstetric glove and run down the barn ally to take a quick peek at Daisy over the stall door.

Inside, it is dim and cool. I turn the thermostat to 60 degrees, and in moments my nostrils are filled with the faint burnt dust smell of the radiant infrared heat coming to life. Thin shafts of sunlight sneak around the edges of the stall doors and under the large overhead doors. Spider, our mama cat, in typical feline form, has claimed the splotch of sunlight high on the fender of the John Deer tractor, where she can oversee her domain.

In Daisy's stall, I place the armload of birthing equipment in a convenient spot, where it will be out of the way but accessible when the time comes. After stroking Daisy's neck for a few minutes, I sit down in a corner to wait until I am needed.

I watch calmly as Daisy circles slowly in discomfort, her hooves churning up pine-scented dust. I find it unexpectedly peaceful in the stall. The pine shavings, a foot and a half deep, hollow comfortably under my butt. I lean back on the cool block wall and feel the infrared heat's feathery touch on my face. My eyes rest on the worn towels with tattered edges, and I smile, recalling when their baby blue softness enfolded my own infant sons, pink and warm from their bath.

Spider, tired of being pestered by Maxx, rises with a queenly stretch. From her perch on top of the block wall, she checks out the action in the stall, her small pink nose twitching, her bright green eyes intent. Daisy starts to lie down, folding her front legs under her, but with a groan, she is up again. Her water breaks. Spider meows softly from her perch. Maxx jumps up. Chin on paws, he peers over the stall door and gets the evil eye from Daisy. She wants nothing to do with his nonsense. She snakes her neck at him, with ears pinned back flat against her head. Maxx easily dodges her. Liking this new game, he immediately jumps back up on the stall—and receives a verbal reprimand from me and two ferocious bats from a hissing cat. Spider's message is clear: This is for mothers only, and you are not welcome. Deeply offended, Maxx lies down; blood beads up on his wet black nose. Distracted by the ruckus, I miss the moment when Daisy delivers a small white hoof.

I am amazed at the slow deliberation with which she lowers her ripe and straining belly to the floor with a drawn-out groan. The wood dust poufs into the air, glinting like gold on beams of sunlight. Watching it swirl around like fairy dust, I think of the magic of this moment, as we three mothers await the arrival of this blessed babe.

Spider jumps into the stall to become part of this divine communion of motherhood. She is a veteran and remembers well the smell of birth and what is to come. A self-appointed comforter, Spider sits at Daisy's head while the dainty mare labors. The cat purrs between contractions, whiskered feline nose touching velvet pony nose, bonded by motherhood. A second white hoof emerges . . . *purr.* A whiskered wet nose . . . *purrrr.* Tiny, chocolate fox ears . . . *purrrrrr.* White shoulders . . . *purrrr-rrrr.* A white chest, dark hips, and light hocks . . . *purrrr-rrrr-rr.*

It's a colt!

The pony lifts her head to see her foal, and then looks to me with new wisdom in her dark liquid eyes. Spider recedes to my lap and begins to wash her snowy paws, but then pauses, catches Daisy's eye, and stares intently at her as if to say, "I purred you through the tricky part, rookie, now you're on your own."

"You're such a good girl," I whisper to Daisy, as I stroke Spider's sleek, ebony fur. "Just look at your handsome, spotted boy."

The foal is vigorous and tries to stand before he is fully delivered. He does an energetic nosedive into the shavings, legs sprawling and spastic. In his struggle for life, he pulls free of Daisy amidst a swirl of golden dust. Rising on wobbling elbows, shavings clinging to him like birthday confetti, he looks at the three of us with cloudy newborn eyes. The colt struggles to focus, blinking his long sticky lashes.

Three pairs of mothering eyes admire him and wait breathlessly for his first steps. Three pairs of ears listen for the first sounds of his voice. Three hearts, at this blessed moment in time, beat only for him. On this day that had no promise, fate has gifted me with a miracle, to be part of this trinity of motherhood: the cat, the pony, and me.

Mary Forseth

A version of this story was first published in Lake Country Journal, *March/April 2006, Evergreen Press, Brainerd, Minnesota.*

The Reunion

When I was thirteen, my father, a professor at the University of Alberta in Edmonton, Canada, announced that he had accepted a job six hundred miles away at the University of Victoria, located on an island off the west coast of Canada. Everyone else was excited, but I faced the news with shock and a thriving sense of dread.

An accelerated program when I was in elementary school had placed me in the unenviable position of being in the ninth grade at the age of thirteen. Daily, I faced the penitentiary of unpopularity, and worse yet, I was regularly ambushed by ridicule. But at least my adversaries were familiar; though my situation was miserable, I knew what to expect. I refused to even think about what I might face in a new school.

The first day of tenth grade found me paralyzed in the front seat of my parents' car, parked
in front of the high school. I wouldn't be fourteen
for another two weeks. I might not have known
what waited within, but I knew everything about me
was wrong. My short boyish haircut, childish clothes,
teeth smothered in braces, and a body more suited
to a pubescent boy than a teenage girl were reasons
enough for me to stay exactly where I was.

"Everything will be all right," my mother said in
an effort to reassure me.

I finally gathered enough courage to enter my
new prison.

The kids were older, which only meant that their
cruelty was more sophisticated and subtle. I trudged
through my days in a blur. My grades were abysmal,
and I skipped out whenever I could. Our new home
was a five-minute walk from the beach, and I spent
hours there, exploring the tidal pools or simply sitting and staring out across the ocean.

Then, one day in homeroom, I overheard a girl
named Nancy talking about horses. I gathered from
what she was saying that she had riding privileges
to an Arabian horse belonging to a friend of her
family's. I also overheard her tell her audience that
the horse was for sale. Heaven only knows what
came over me, but during a lull in the conversation,

I joined the discussion. "I'm looking for a horse to buy," I said and proceeded to tell the group that had gathered an elaborate fabrication about my vast experience with horses, particularly Arabians.

I had been horse crazy for years, but I had never considered the possibility of having one of my own. Nancy gave me a piece of paper with the name and phone number of the horse's owner. "Give him a call," she urged.

I walked home that day rehearsing the speech I would use on my parents in an effort to convince them I needed a horse. I knew this scheme would require more than one request, so I plotted my strategy. I composed answers to every possible question and objection my parents might have.

A firm and emphatic "No!" greeted my first proposal. Never mind that my father worked long hours at his new job; every night he found the "Horses for Sale" column from the newspaper classified ads on his pillow along with a picture of Gabriel—the horse I wanted to buy—and a list of the remarkable and unique characteristics of the Arabian breed. I drove my mother and anyone else who would listen to distraction talking about horses.

I wanted Gabriel to satisfy my passion for horses, but I also somehow knew that he would be my saving grace, the miracle that would rescue me from the lonely and wretched feelings that haunted me. I would have a purpose, something to look forward to, and a reason to get through the school day. I never shared these feelings with my parents. In fact, I had never told them about my situation at school. I realize now that my secrecy was in vain. Not only were they aware of my problems, but, unbeknownst to me, they were giving serious consideration to buying Gabriel for the very reasons I was reluctant to express.

Then one magical night, my father phoned Gabriel's owner and arranged to buy him. And because dreams do come true, Gabriel fulfilled all the hopes I had harbored. I spent every spare minute in his company, and I made friends with the other girls who kept their horses at the same boarding stable. Nothing changed at school, but Gabriel became my buffer. For four years, he was the love of my life.

I was in my third year of university when I had to face a difficult, almost unthinkable, decision. My studies took up an inordinate amount of my time, and it wouldn't be long before I would be leaving my hometown to teach school. When my riding teacher told me she had met someone who wanted to buy Gabriel, I discussed the matter with my parents. They told me they would agree with whatever I decided, but I felt guilty. Upkeep for a horse stayed the same whether or not he was ridden, and my parents were still spending a lot of money on something for which I no longer had time.

One day, the man who wanted to buy Gabriel showed up at the riding stable with his two young children. They rode Gabriel and loved him. I could find no fault with the family as potential owners, but I felt like I was selling my best friend. I put Gabriel back in his stall and accepted the man's check, waiting to cry until I was alone. I went back to the stable once to collect my tack, but I couldn't bring myself to ever say goodbye. My interest in horses waned as I grieved, and I didn't ride again for a long time.

Some years later, I found myself sharing an apartment with a good friend named Maggie. I had moved back to the West Coast and had been unable to find another teaching position. So, like Maggie, I worked for the government. One day, she came home with a big grin on her face. She teased me briefly with the promise of a surprise and finally admitted something I could scarcely believe. That day she had met a woman named Kate who owned several horses, one of which was a fifteen-year-old Arabian gelding named Gabriel. I began to tremble and tears filled my eyes.

Maggie grasped my hands. "What are you waiting for?" she asked, still smiling. "I've got the address, and Kate is expecting us."

I rushed to the fridge and grabbed a bag of carrots. On the way to Kate's farm, Maggie filled me in on Gabriel's history since he had left my care. The daughter of the man who had bought him had suffered a bad fall that resulted in Gabriel being sold once again. When Kate found him, he had been abandoned in a field, undernourished and ill. She restored him to health and told Maggie he now had a home for the rest of his life. It broke my heart to think of him suffering through such difficult times, but I rejoiced that Kate had found him.

Before I knew it, we were pulling into a driveway. I saw fenced pastures and barns, but no Gabriel. I turned to Maggie. "I'm scared," I said. "What if he's changed? What if he doesn't know me?"

"Come on," she said, opening her car door. "You'll never know if you stay here."

A woman came out of the house and introduced herself as Kate. I liked her right away. "Come on in the house and have a cold drink," she said, but when she saw my face, she laughed. "You're not interested in a drink, are you? I don't blame you one bit." She gestured to a pasture behind one of the barns. "Gabriel is out there, somewhere. There's a halter hanging on the gate. You can bring him up to the house if you want. You can even have a ride."

I stood there for a moment, feeling like a fool with my plastic bag full of carrots. As if reading my mind, Kate said, "He hasn't changed a bit. He may be a bit too fat, but he's healthy and happy. You go ahead and have a nice, long visit." She beckoned to Maggie. "We'll be waiting up at the house when you're done."

I watched them walk away and started toward the pasture. I looked in vain for Gabriel, and then suddenly he was there. I called his name softly, my voice shaky and hesitant. He continued grazing, and I called him again, this time with confidence. He looked up and whinnied. The years slipped away as he ambled toward me, eying my bag of carrots and making the sweet, snuffling sound I knew so well.

I gently took hold of a handful of his mane, as I always used to do, and led him back to the gate. There, I slipped on the halter Kate had given me and threw the rope over his neck. I found a stump and climbed onto his back. He moved forward expectantly, but I pulled him to a stop. I couldn't believe what was happening. There I was, sitting on Gabriel's back. All I could do was throw my arms around his neck, bury my face in his mane, and inhale the sweet smell I remembered as well as my own name.

Susan B. Townsend

A Sensational Contract

The beast was huge, charged with murderous intent, and bearing down on me from behind. The faster I went, the closer he came. With a huff, he blew air through his nostrils, and I could feel the warmth stirring the hair on my neck. Terrified, I started to run. Choking on the dust kicked up by his tremendous hooves, I raced toward the safety of the gate and flung myself through the uneven boards of the fence, the thundering hooves behind me sliding to an abrupt halt.

Falling against the big gate of the corral for support, my sister laughed, gasping for air and wiping her eyes. "Amy, you're leading him by the reins. When you race around like a scared spider, he has to run to keep up."

I looked down at the strips of leather clutched between my fingers and then at the fearless marauder who had shrunk suddenly into a tiny pony with neatly trimmed hooves and an overgrown mane. He sighed and stamped one small foot to shoo away a pesky fly. If horses could die of boredom, he'd be joining the ghost riders in the sky any second.

A shy, scrawny tomboy of a kid, I was all bones and bruises and blonde hair—with the grace and self-confidence of an eggplant. In my mind, this incident was just another example of my awkwardness, another thing to feel insecure about.

Kerry paid for the hour of equine appreciation and gave the pony a final pat. "Who knew this little fellow was a stalker?" she quipped with glee.

Later, as she turned the car out of the dusty driveway, I looked back through the billowing clouds of dirt for one last look at the monster that had tripled my adrenalin output. A small, brown, innocent face peered back at me over the fence.

That's it! I thought. *One day I'm going to learn to ride a horse.*

Ten years later, and with me having made no more progress toward conquering my fear, we added a sweetheart of a retired show horse to the family. I peered up into a gigantic pair of moist nostrils above a smudge of chestnut fuzz that resembled a well-groomed mustache. His name: A Sensational Contract. Right. If "sensational" meant big enough to knock me across the stall with a single toss of his Roman nose, he had the right name. Luckily he was more interested in searching my pockets for treats than pressing his size advantage.

Because Kerry would soon leave to earn her Horsemaster's Certificate in the comfort and safety of a New England academy, I was apprenticed to the treacherous job of groom and babysitter to a half-ton of flyaway hair and a panoramic mouthful of big teeth. The enormous horse lowered his huge muzzle onto the top of my head and nuzzled my scalp. He either approved of me or liked my apple-scented shampoo.

For someone who doesn't ride, exercising a saddlebred is a lot like coursing down a snowy slope without skis. By then, at least, I was comfortable going into the stall, stirring up clouds of dust and hair with a curry comb and dandy brush. And when I cleaned his hooves and he bent his big head around to give me a friendly nuzzle, I usually didn't even squeal.

I made sure he got plenty of fresh air and pasture time, and sometimes I would tease him into some extra exercise by turning him out in the riding ring and running laps outside the wooden fence while holding his favorite treat, a cold grape soda, in the air like an Olympic torch. We would run in large loopy circles until I collapsed, giggling, against the wooden fence and let him have a long drink. He would hang his head over my shoulder in a horsey hug, and I would wrap my arms around his big neck and nuzzle my face against his warm body.

On rainy days, when both end doors of the big barn were closed, Seet—his nickname, baby talk for "sweet"—would trot up and down the sawdust aisle, peeking in the stalls of other horses not fortunate enough to be out for a scamper. Once when I left him alone long enough to buy a drink from the machine in the lounge, he helped himself to a hearty snack from the feed room. Without a thought, I squeezed past the fuzzy hindquarters filling the doorway to give him a stern lecture on grain theft. He had the presence of mind to look embarrassed as I led him back to his stall.

Often, some of the other boarders at the stable would call to me as they set off on a ride through cool woods of the countryside. "We're trail riding. Want to go?"

I would mumble a reply and shake my head. Later, when they would return laughing about the adventures of the trail, I would wonder if learning to ride would be like learning to ride a bike. The first time I'd taken off without training wheels, I had collided with the house, relocated my handlebars, and ripped the blooms from my mother's favorite bed of tiger lilies. If the brakes fail on horseback, there's more to lose than the first blooms of the season.

Kerry came back from horse school with enthusiasm bursting at the seams of her jodhpurs, determined to try out her newfound knowledge. Would education translate into real-life experience?

As I stood safely on the ground measuring the distance to the saddle in much the same way an alpine adventurer gauges his trip up the mountain and decides to wait for a better day, a warm nose nudged me from behind. If the horse was that confident, the least I could do was give it a try. I sighed, put one foot in the stirrup, and looked up. It appeared to be an altogether unstable environment. There certainly weren't any training wheels in sight.

Fortunately, since I wasn't an exceptionally fine student, this was an exceptionally fine horse. He couldn't have been calmer if he had been catnapping. While memories of a stalker pony stampeded through my head, my sister said the strangest thing.

"Don't worry. He won't let you fall off."

Surveying the world from a dizzying height of perhaps five feet from the ground, I doubted her wisdom and questioned her integrity. My mount sighed and dozed off. Checking his commitment, I leaned to one side. He shifted his weight to maintain a firm foundation underneath my body. Concentrating on grape sodas and afternoon hugs, I gave him a gentle squeeze. He began to walk slowly around the ring. I dropped my weight into the saddle, trying to remember all of Kerry's instructions at once. We finished a crooked circle and started on the second. I could ride this horse!

It took several lessons, but it seemed like no time had passed until we were trotting right along. One day as we headed back to the barn, Seet stumbled over an unexpected dip in the ground. Before I had time to panic, he was surefooted again, shifting his weight to make sure he didn't lose his passenger.

Eventually, Kerry and I ventured out on trail rides through the countryside just like I had seen the other folks do. We took leisurely trips that allowed for deep breaths of country air and plenty of time to admire the patchwork pattern of local pastures. One day we rode past a fence where a pony was snacking on mouthfuls of tasty grass. My thoughts galloped back over the years to the little brown stalker pony, and I grinned. That little fellow started me down the bridle path, but it took A Sensational Contract to teach me to ride. As it turned out, the only thing too big about him was his heart.

Amy Ammons Mullis

The Starting Line

I paced the kitchen, fingers wrapped around my cooling coffee cup, tears spilling down my face. It was over. The thing that I had dreaded for so long had finally happened.

I had watched my good old horse, Barry, go from a vital, energetic senior gentleman to a tired old man—it seemed nearly overnight—as some illness that we could not completely diagnose ate away at him. The veterinarian visited him so many times I lost count. Scopes, blood tests, drugs, special diets—nothing seemed to put weight on Barry. We couldn't bring back the lively, eccentric spirit that had once been his defining personality characteristic. I watched him grow thinner and quieter, a little bit more each day.

Winter was approaching, and terrified that the cold weather would cause him needless suffering,

I agonized about whether I should put him down. Then, like the gallant friend he had always been, he took matters into his own hands. On a warm afternoon, under a cloudless, turquoise autumn sky, he lay down in the field and refused to rise again. The vet came and put him humanely to sleep.

For a while, I just mourned Barry. I took a bag of deer apples out to the stable for the horse buddies he had left behind. I fetched his ashes from the university where his body was cremated and buried them in my side yard. I put a few hairs from his tail in my jewelry box.

Visiting the barn without my own horse there to tend felt odd, and I finally began to consider what to do next. I was, for the first time in nearly thirty-five years, without an equine companion. My emotions were mixed—a combination of relief, anticipation, worry, and grief. As Barry had worsened, my thoughts had inevitably turned to what horse I might find to replace him when he was gone. But I could not make that decision while he was still alive, so I'd simply formed a mental list of musings and then set it aside to consider later. It was time to reinvent that list.

The possibilities seemed endless. Purchase a show horse? A trail horse? A talented dressage animal? Turn my energies to some other style of riding? Try a breed I had always admired? Perhaps a Lipizzaner or an Andalusian?

Or perhaps no horse at all?

My mind balked at the idea of being horseless. I owned horses since I was sixteen years old. I identified myself as a horse-owner, looked at horse art, sported horse jewelry, counted myself among the horse-crazed multitudes that swarm equine trade shows and stand for hours by fences at show practice rings, watching the horses canter and trot, circle and halt, back and walk on.

But lately my family, career, home, and myriad other interests were making horse time increasingly precious. My practical side asked: *If I can't make time to ride as I did when I was in my twenties, is a horse really for me?* Barry as a senior citizen was past the need for training or long hours spent with an instructor. I wasn't sure where I would find the time for a new, young horse. Had I moved on to some other stage in my life?

A friend called me. Had I checked with a particular trainer up north, she asked. The trainer had a nice mare for sale, trained to fourth-level dressage.

I checked my mental list and noted the entry for a talented dressage animal. Though I made the telephone call, I didn't go up to see the horse. The time issue was still looming, but something else was bothering me more—a disquieting thought about the coming years. I realized that if I purchased a young animal now, it could very well be the last horse I would ever own. This time I would be growing old along with my horse. Perhaps, rather than the Lipizzaner or the spirited Warmblood I had always dreamed about, I should be looking for a placid animal that would carry me safely into my retirement.

I thought back to the years I had owned Barry and the horses before him. Those were the days of my youth. Days of college, of marriage, of my daughter as a baby and then as a young girl, of travel to a new home, of new friends. Days of dressage lessons, jumping lessons, trail rides, overnight trips to shows, and riding clinics. Of new opportunities, new chances, a million doors open before me, a million horses to ride.

And now? Suddenly, all the new beginnings seemed to be behind me. I smiled wanly at myself. I found a certain dark humor in the idea that I seemed to be in the midst of a midlife crisis associated with horses. I fretted and pondered, but did not go looking for a new horse.

Then one day my phone rang. It was the woman who owned the farm where Barry had lived.

"Have you checked out CANTER?" she asked.

CANTER, the Communication Alliance to Network Thoroughbred Ex-Racehorses, is a nonprofit volunteer organization whose goal is to provide retiring racehorses with opportunities for new lives. I was intrigued. I have always felt my humane society dogs and cats made the most satisfactory companions, and I liked the idea of helping a horse that needed to find a new home.

I went to the CANTER Web site and was astounded at the pages and pages of available horses. The track was closing for the season, and many trainers were looking to place animals that were no longer succeeding on the racetrack. With the first real enthusiasm I'd felt since Barry died, I began to review the available horses. I decided to look for a gelding, five years or older, smaller than Barry's 16.2 hands. I still had two pages of options. To limit the results further, I sorted them by color. I had always been partial to grays.

And there he was. Silver Blur, a six-year-old Thoroughbred gelding, 15.1 hands, steel gray.

With no idea what to expect, my daughter, my friend Jan, and I drove the two hours to the track to see Silver Blur. The visit was comical in many regards. We weren't allowed to ride outside for liability reasons, and I neglected to take my own saddle with me, so I had to ride Silver Blur in a racing saddle down the barn aisle while the other racehorses looked on. Some simply hung their heads out of their stalls to watch, while others lunged at us, teeth bared, as we sidled cautiously by. I felt it was a tribute to my mount's disposition that we finished that ride without any major disasters. I know I felt like quite a spectacle with my legs all pretzeled into the short stirrups. If horses could snicker, I'm sure several of them were doing just that.

"He has a knob on his right fore," Jan pointed out as we walked around Blur, inspecting from all angles.

She was right. He did have a knob—quite a large one—on his ankle. A racing injury, the groom told me. Blur had also been pinfired on his forelegs, I saw, indicating he'd probably had another injury. There was no real guarantee he would remain sound after I bought him.

But I kept watching his face. He craned his neck to stare out at some distant point, his black eyes bright and his ears pricked. What was he looking at? A passing car? Another horse out on the track? Or was he remembering some finish line he would never again cross and wondering what was beyond it? I tried to look where he was looking, but I couldn't tell.

A few moments later Blur dropped his head, and I put out my hand. He inspected it for a moment, as if unsure what was expected of him. If it had been Barry, he would have searched for a treat—a carrot or a peppermint. But this was a racehorse, unaccustomed to being fawned over and spoiled. I felt the delicate brush of his whiskers and a warm whuff as he blew out a quizzical breath. Then he lowered his nose, and my horse nuzzled my fingers for the first time.

Loraine J. Hudson

More Than a Horse, of Course

I was lucky to begin riding in my mid-teens on a wonderful Thoroughbred named Summer Bee. Summer Bee was big and muscular—a solid 16.2 hands, with large feet, a broad back, and a double mane. He was a tough racehorse and a breeding stallion—not the kind of horse recommended for a sixteen-year-old girl who weighed 100 pounds and had taken only a few riding lessons. But somehow he was the perfect horse for me.

I rode him all over the small town where I grew up. I'd ride him double with my friend Carol. I'd take him up behind the school and park him under the monkey bars, then climb the bars and lower myself back into the saddle. One of my favorite rides was through the huge industrial park and down the old railroad tracks by the dump. The track's rails and ties had long since been pulled up, leaving a straight dirt path. I would ride Summer Bee far down the "tracks," then I'd turn him and gallop toward home. He ran so fast my eyes watered and the wind roared in my ears. It took only the word "easy" to slow him down and "whoa" to bring him to a complete stop.

Summer Bee did whatever I asked and was always calm and steady. Over the two years I was fortunate to ride him wherever and whenever I wanted, he also showed me how incredibly smart he was. But the most amazing thing he ever did probably saved my life.

One day Carol and I were both riding Summer Bee through a short stretch of woods when suddenly Summer Bee stopped and stood dead still. I urged him on, to no avail. Figuring he sensed danger in the woods, I got off and led him past the "danger" spot. As soon as I tried to remount, he made it clear he wasn't going to let me back in the saddle. He did nothing dramatic. He just stood perfectly still, until I went to put my foot in the stirrup, and then he'd take one step away. Normally, Summer Bee stood like a statue, and he was huge. That one step back was as scary as any other horse rearing and flipping over backward.

After a few attempts, both Carol and I were too afraid to do anything but return to the barn. When I took off the saddle, the mystery was solved. As I lifted the flap to undo the girth I saw that one of the two elastic straps was completely severed, frayed from old age, and the other one was hanging by a few elastic bands. Summer Bee must have felt the girth break. If the saddle had slid, I could have fallen under an eighteen-wheeler in the industrial park or hit the ground at 40 miles an hour during a mad gallop down the tracks. What a horse! I was so proud of him.

The next year Summer Bee returned to racing. He had not been in much demand as a stallion, and because horses were a business for his owner, Summer Bee had to earn his keep. He again proved how special he was by winning—even after a two-year layoff. I was heartbroken when he was later sold. And I was certain I would never be lucky enough to find another horse as wonderful as he had been.

During the twenty-five years following my last ride on Summer Bee, I owned several horses, worked at the track, became a licensed racehorse trainer, did a stint as a farm manager, and was a trail guide in Missouri. I, indeed, found other horses as wonderful as Summer Bee—different, but just as wonderful.

Then, I gave up horses for about ten years to raise my sons. When I was fifty-one, I was again able to fit a horse into my life and I rescued one. Then, several months later, I decided I wanted a horse to ride. Every day on my way to where my rescued horse was boarded, I passed a Paint breeding farm. Curious, I stopped in one day to see what they had for sale.

Well, there were plenty of horses! I was left alone in a herd of about thirty, most with great conformation. They were all fillies and mares, except for two— the owner's riding horse and a black gelding with a white spot above his tail. The gelding was striking-looking, but he had a long back and his butt was higher than his withers. I confess to being somewhat of a snob; used to Thoroughbreds, I could not bring myself to consider a horse with poor conformation.

Then my life changed forever. The gelding faced me head-on, and I heard him say "me." I actually responded out loud, saying, "No, not you." Thankfully, I was alone and no one could hear me.

I turned away and began a closer examination of a couple of the mares. Out of the corner of my eye I could see the gelding snake his way through the herd until he was again facing me head-on and again I heard "me." I turned away with another "not you," wondering if I were getting senile.

I tried to check out another horse, but once again, the black horse made his way through all the mares until he and I ended up face-to-face a third time. "Me!" Begrudgingly I said "fine." Had a horse really just talked me into buying him?

I paid for the gelding, whose registered name was Mighty Tippy Too. At least I dickered and managed to lower the price by $400. I still couldn't believe I'd bought him. When I returned to pick him up, the owner's husband informed me (I hadn't even thought to ask!) that he was barely broken, having had only a handful of rides a few years earlier. He was now six! This was an unwelcome shock. I was over fifty; I wanted a quiet, dead-broke horse. What had I been thinking? Worse, the horse had bucked off the son-in-law! Oh great.

The next day I put him on the lunge line and found out he'd never done that before, either. But he seemed cooperative and quickly got the basic hang of it. The following day I decided to saddle him up and see what happened. He took it all in stride, never batting an eye. Encouraged, I lunged him with the saddle on, and he was fine. The third day I repeated the lunging with the saddle. Huey, as I called him, was very good. Very relaxed. Very calm. I decided to see what he'd do if I tried to mount. . . . Nothing. That was positive. I not only got on him that day and rode him, but by the end of the week I actually hauled to the Devil's Backbone trail and rode him! Aside from being very green and barely able to steer, he acted like he'd done it his whole life.

Huey was a friendly, intelligent horse, and he was very interested in humans. He especially liked to stand quietly, as if listening, while I talked with other people. I kept thinking about how he had talked me into buying him. I ended up having an animal communicator talk to him, and his reading jibed with what I had experienced. Mighty-Huey actually wanted to be my horse!

I've long believed that horses are much more intelligent than most people give them credit for. While I felt I had a "knack" for getting along with them, I never really thought about animal-human communication before. But after the way Huey had gotten me to buy him and the reading, I was a believer. As I thought about all the amazing experiences I'd had with other horses, I realized that I had been communicating with them—and they with me. I suddenly remembered several instances in which my horses had seemed amazingly brilliant and done exactly the right thing—usually, a very nonhorsey thing. Then it struck me: in every instance, I'd had a very clear mental image of what I wanted to happen, and somehow they had tuned into it.

For a while after the communicator confirmed that Huey had chosen me, I couldn't even bring myself to ride him. But Huey quickly made it clear that he missed riding, so I got over it. Still, I have never been able to bring myself to "train" Huey in the way I trained horses before. It seemed demeaning in a way, at least with Huey. So, though I have ridden Huey for five years now. I have never ridden him with a bit. We just get along. He does what I ask him to do because he wants to. He has, in fact, always acted as though he wants to be with me.

I have "heard" Huey on several occasions, and he has demonstrated his exceptional intelligence many times—but none more dramatically than when he and the rest of my herd all got loose.

After an hour-long chase, I finally managed to get a halter on Huey and then on Lucy, my usual lead horse, and was walking the herd home. Because Huey is herd leader, the other four horses were coming along behind him. I was nearly home when a woman pulled over and offered to help. When we came to a 90-degree bend in the road, I became concerned. The road dips, and anyone in the road is not visible to traffic approaching the bend from the direction we were heading. I took Huey and Lucy and jogged ahead. I got to the corner just in time. I waved my arms, and the car slowed down. Then I visualized stepping from the shoulder into the street to make sure the car saw us and stopped. As soon as I took one step forward, Huey grabbed my shoulder in his teeth! I was so stunned it actually took a full second for me to figure out what happened. Huey had never even nibbled, much less bitten, anyone. I turned around and hit him.

I knew immediately that he had seen my thoughts—seen me stepping directly into the path of the car. And he had done the only thing he could to stop me. I apologized to him for my stupidity and vowed never again to hit him without thinking first.

Words cannot even describe how badly I felt. In an attempt to make it up to him, the next day I took him out to hand-graze on the grass by the driveway. At some point I turned away, and to my utter shock, Huey bit me! Very gently. But when I looked at him, I could see the laughter in his eyes, as though he were saying, "Just testing."

Many people—probably most—will no doubt scoff that it was all my imagination. But I don't believe that for a second. And anyone who has experienced the magic that is horse knows that sometimes horses and humans really do know what the other is thinking. The horse is a special animal, a gift from God. Beautiful and powerful, intelligent and free-spirited. Built perfectly for us to ride, the horse willingly becomes our partner and is more easily trained than our beloved dogs. I believe horses have much to teach us—if we open our minds and hearts and listen.

Maureen Gould

A version of this story was first published under the title "My Horses, My Friends" in Natural Horse Magazine, *July/August 2006.*

That's Love

"I'm so glad you came with me today," Tricia said to me as she tied her chestnut horse, Cody, to one side of the trailer.

I knew she didn't mean it. The anticipation of riding on some of the best local trails was not enough to make me forget that my nickname at the barn was the "crazy Paso Fino lady." My friendship with Tricia stemmed more from convenience than mutual appreciation. Tricia didn't like to ride alone, and I didn't have my own trailer.

I unloaded Scooter. At 13.3 hands, he was often dismissed as a pony, but with a toss of his mane and a stomp of his hooves he would dispute the label. In Scooter's heart, he was a horse.

Despite the bravado, Scooter stood patiently while I secured his lead to the trailer. His brio was often confused with defiance at the barn, but Scooter was a gentle soul. In the two years I had owned him, he had yet to let me down. I wanted a horse I could be myself with: fast when I wanted fast, mellow when I wanted to relax. I had no interest in taking lessons; instead, I wanted a horse I could have fun with.

Warm Sunday afternoons were all about playing baseball from Scooter's back while my husband and children raced around imaginary bases. Sometimes we'd simply gallop on the rail like it was a racetrack and then relax with a picnic in the shade. Scooter would close his eyes and rock back and forth with a child reclining on his back as we ate.

I suppose it was no surprise the other owners had nicknames for me. They were very serious horse-women who practiced often to win ribbons they displayed with pride. We didn't have much in common. Even for this trail ride, Tricia was impeccably dressed. The design on her breeches matched her jacket and helmet. I looked down self-consciously at my faded jeans and tattered barn boots, but then shook it off and continued to tack up. Sunshine and lack of mud were far more important than our differences in riding attire.

I had just secured Scooter's saddle when I heard Cody begin to stomp wildly on the other side of the trailer. I left Scooter's side just in time to see Tricia's horse pull back and break the clip that tied him to the trailer. He bounced onto his back and then scrambled to his feet and took off across the field.

The field was mostly enclosed by bushes and fencing, but at the far corner of the field a large gate led to a main road. The gate was open to allow trailers to enter the park, and Cody was heading straight for it. I looked around quickly. Other riders were tacking up, but no one was ready. I jumped on Scooter's back, hoping I had secured the saddle enough. I knew I had to beat Cody to that driveway and turn him back. There was no time for reins. Scooter's halter and the lead line would have to do.

As if reading my mind, Scooter lowered his head and set off after Cody in a full gallop. As we closed in on the big horse, a moment of sanity intruded: Without reins, I'd have no way of stopping Scooter when we reached the gate. There was a very good chance I would be an unwilling participant in a wild ride down the road with both horses.

We passed Cody, who was still heading toward the gate. I dug one hand into Scooter's mane and prayed that he understood my goal.

When Scooter was a good distance in front of the quarter horse, he suddenly turned and stopped. I almost flew off, but clung to his neck. Righting myself, I realized Scooter had stopped just shy of the exit. He braced himself as the other horse thundered toward us. At the last moment, Cody turned and headed back toward the trailers.

Cody ran himself out in the remaining enclosed area. When he tired, Tricia caught him with ease.

Scooter and I rode slowly back to the trailer. I wanted to jump down and hug him, but my legs were still shaking. I had always considered Scooter a member of my family, but that day was a testament of his loyalty to me. He could have chosen to follow his instincts and run off with the other horse. Instead, he understood my goal and put himself in danger to achieve it. That's not training. That's love.

Tricia hugged me when I dismounted. "I knew as soon as I saw you jump on Scooter that Cody was going to be okay," she said. "I knew you could bring him back."

I felt a little ashamed then. I had been wrong about Tricia. We could be friends, after all, despite our differences.

"So what do you think?" she asked. "Are you still up for a ride?"

My smile mirrored the one on her face. "Hell, yes!"

No matter how the day had started, sunshine and lack of mud were far more important to two horsewomen spoiling for a ride.

Ruth Cardello

A Horse-Shopping Adventure

This is how it is with horse people: When you're shopping for a horse, your friends always want to help. My friend Carol is no different. I no sooner get the words "I want to buy a horse" out of my mouth than she's on it, searching high and low for "a good horse" for me. What she finds is an ad for a nineteen-year-old Morgan mare, "reasonably priced," "looking for a good home."

That sounds good. We call the number and make an appointment to see the mare. When we arrive at the address, the horse is tied to a tree outside a small barn and bucking like a rodeo bronc. We parked and sit in stunned silence, watching her buck.

Finally I say, "Let's go."

"We should at least say 'no thanks' to the man," Carol says, pointing to the guy who's just stepped out of the barn.

It seems to me that racing furiously backward out of the driveway and spewing gravel halfway down the road would communicate exactly what I want to say: "Thanks for wasting my time, you jerk!" Carol has better manners than I do. So I say, "Okay, you go tell him 'hi, no thanks,' and I'll watch from the farm next door. Just don't get near that horse!"

"No problem!" she agrees, laughing. "Come on," she says, "get out."

As I emerge from the vehicle, I cautiously watch the still-bucking horse, thinking, *At any moment, she's gonna break that tie, and it's every woman for herself!*

The man's name is Tom. I'm too distracted by his wild horse to catch his last name.

I gesture toward the mare. "Is she always like that?" *And how the heck do you expect to sell a horse like that?* is my next thought.

"Oh no," Tom replies.

He has red hair and is wearing a polo shirt and slacks. *Not really a cowboy,* I think.

"She's a good horse," Tom assures us. "Just a little excited."

Well, that's an understatement, I think.

Then I say, "She's not what we're looking for," and start walking back to the car.

"Wait! Don't you want to ride her?" Tom asks.

"Are you crazy?" I snap, not pausing to find my manners. "No thanks!"

"But she's really nice to ride," he almost pleads.

I look at him, narrow my eyes, and put my hands on my hips. "You ride her first," I say in a low voice, a dare.

"Sure!" Tom smiles and hurries back into the barn. He returns a few moments later with a saddle and bridle. He has a little trouble getting the saddle on the mare, who is still hopping around the tree. But when he finally gets the thing on her back, she settles down and allows him to tighten the cinch. Then he unties her from the tree and bridles her without a problem.

I hold my breath while Tom draws the reins over the mare's head. She stands perfectly still as Tom swings up into the saddle. Then he turns her and trots down the driveway. Up and down the driveway they go, and then down the road and back. Tom dismounts. He has good manners: he doesn't say a word, only smiles and hands the reins to me.

I manage to close my mouth, which I realize has been hanging open, and get up into the saddle, certain even as I do that the mare has saved all her bucking for me. But the horse has manners, too. We trot up and down the driveway, then down the road and back. She trots happily and stops obediently when asked. I head back to Tom, dismount, and keep hold of the reins.

"Why did she buck so much before?" I ask.

"Well, I should have told you," Tom says with a big grin. He's enjoying the moment. "This is my daughter's horse. She lost interest in riding—discovered boys, you know—and this mare's been standing in her stall for three months, because we don't have a pasture. So I finally put my foot down and told my daughter I was selling her horse. Today was the first time the mare has been outside in three months."

I bought the mare. She never bucked again. And she never again stayed in a stall for three months. Eventually, I learned some manners, too.

Charlotte Godfrey

I Dreamt of Horses

I dreamt of horses the other night, bringing the nearly forgotten essence of them with me into wakefulness. Of all the difficulties I have faced since my accident, the loss of my horses has always seemed the hardest, but I'm getting ahead of myself. Let me start at the beginning.

For as long as I can remember, I have had the soul of a horsewoman. In my youth, thanks to a benevolent and doting grandmother, I was given the opportunity to own, ride, and show hunters. My horses were the reason I got out of bed each day. They put the smile on my face and the joy in my step. I spent as much time as possible at the barn, even after reaching my teens, when young boys began to catch my eye. Nothing touched me like the smell of sweet hay on a cold winter's morn or the gentle tickle of whiskers and soft breath on my neck. The essence of equine that flooded my senses whenever I buried my face in my mare's neck—her sleek coat beneath my fingers, the warmth of her body, her incomparable fragrance—that, to me, was perfect happiness.

Unfortunately, my childhood bliss did not transition gradually into adult pleasure; it came to an abrupt and shattering end. One day, just two weeks after my sixteenth birthday, I broke my neck diving into our backyard pool. In an instant, I became a quadriplegic, paralyzed from the chest down. I spent the next three months in a local hospital and the following six months at a rehab hospital in New York City. I didn't truly grasp how much my life had changed until the day I came home from New York to find that my parents had removed everything equine from my life. My tack was gone, my ribbons and trophies removed from my room, and the most crushing blow of all, my precious mare had been sold. That was the lowest moment of my life.

The young are resilient, though, and I refused to let my wheelchair limit my outlook on life. I pulled myself up by my bootstraps and finished high school. Then I left my childhood home in Pittsford, New York, to attend college in Miami, Florida. I did all the things "normal" young women did back in the sixties. I even went to equine events occasionally, but the horses seemed huge and intimidating to me.

I couldn't believe that I now feared what had once been so dear.

After I graduated from the University of Miami, I met an amazing young man who accepted me for who I was and didn't care about the things I couldn't do. Kip and I were married within six months. We quickly made a home for ourselves and were blessed with two beautiful sons. Our life was not always easy. Being a full-time caregiver was often difficult for my husband, and pressure sores and various infections landed me in the hospital time and time again. But, all things considered, my life was sweet.

Some nights, however, I still awoke to bittersweet memories of the horses I loved, and I could smell the faint ghostly fragrance of sweet hay as I lay there alone with my thoughts. Though I would always be a quadriplegic, I still had a horsewoman's soul.

One brilliant summer day, my family started out on one of our traditional, leisurely Sunday drives, but once we were on the road, my husband announced we were going on a house-hunting expedition. We'd been looking for a larger home ever since the boys were babies, but we had recently gotten serious about buying. The boys had grown and needed more room to run and play outside, and my husband had always wanted a home in the country.

Kip pulled off the narrow rural road onto a drive flanked by evergreens, and the first thing I saw was a small barn nestled behind a house. To this day I cannot remember my first glimpse of the house, even though I know that's what I should have focused on. I should have looked it over thoroughly to see if it was wheelchair accessible. I should have looked to see if it had good-sized bedrooms for the boys. I should have looked to see if it was a good fit for our family. But my heart wasn't in the house . . . it was out in that little gem of a barn.

We finally ended our inspection of the house and made our way outside. The boys took off toward the remains of an overgrown orchard, which had a couple of trees that looked to hold great climbing potential, and I finally turned my attention to the barn. A level path led from the horseshoe driveway to the open double doors of the barn, an easy journey for my power chair. I felt as giddy as a girl as I made my way down the path, my husband close behind. I slowed upon leaving the warm, bright sunlight and entering the cool, dim barn—and then stopped. I let the unforgettable aroma of leather, hay, and horses wash over me while my eyes adjusted to the darkness. Kip joined me, and we shared a perfect moment of silence at the barn entrance. I knew he understood how difficult my exile had been. Our silence was broken by a soft rustling and a small, gentle nicker. My eyes flew to my husband's face, and when our eyes met, I realized he had that silly grin on his face that was a sure sign he'd been keeping a huge secret.

Confusion gave way to comprehension, which immediately turned to disbelief. I tore my gaze from Kip's face and peered eagerly into the depth of the barn. My heart stood still when I saw the dainty, perfectly proportioned, wheelchair-sized horse standing in one of the miniature stalls that had been built in the center of the barn. My eyes brimmed with tears as I took in her sable coat, her sparkling white mane and tail, and her huge, liquid eyes.

My amazing husband went and opened the stall door. He clipped a lead with a loop on the end onto her halter and brought her over to me. He slipped the loop onto my thumb and kissed me sweetly. I barely heard his simple, understated explanation: "I'm putting an offer in on the house. The horse is for sale, too. Do you want her?"

My tears spilled over then, tumbling over the tremulous smile that had appeared on my face. I was unable to speak. The joy of this unexpected gift was overwhelming. As I gazed into my husband's eyes, I knew there was no need for words, so I slowly turned and led my elegant little mare toward the sunshine. When we reached the doorway, I stopped to savor the sweet, familiar scent of hay and horses once again. At that moment I felt the gentle tickle of whiskers exploring my cheek and soft breath on my neck. I wrapped my arms around her, totally unafraid, and buried my face in her neck. My heart was full.

I dreamt of horses again that night, bringing the newly remembered essence of them with me into wakefulness. My dream was no longer bittersweet; it was filled with overflowing love for one small, sweet mare and with the hope that some day my barn would be full. I'd found perfect happiness once again. My soul was complete.

Nancy L. Gillen

All Little Girls Love Horses

She arrived on a gray Michigan afternoon to much oohing and ahing. My brother Brian and his wife, Mary, had waited almost two years for a child to adopt. Their first child, my parents' first grandchild, and my first (and to date, only) niece, came on Thanksgiving Day.

That night, my other sister-in-law, Erin, gushed, "Don't you just love Maddy?"

In nature, parents fall in love with their offspring quickly. It helps perpetuate the species. I'm not a parent. Love her? I didn't even know her. And quite frankly, when I held her, the thought occurred to me that any number of newborn mammals would win a Cute Baby Contest over this wrinkled creature.

I was thirty-four when Maddy arrived on November 22, 2000. I never had the desire to breed, then or now. Children are fine as long as they are somebody else's.

Horses . . . now, that's another matter.

Glenwood Avenue in southeast Grand Rapids, Michigan, is a tree-lined street in a middle-class, urban neighborhood with solid, stucco, vintage 1930s homes. I grew up there in the 1970s. Horses were as far away to me as the moon.

I remember feeling jealous of my father because, as a youngster growing up on a farm, he had a faithful old blind Paint named Scout—a gift from his parents.

I remember drawing horses. Over and over, I would copy the one galloping on the cover of *By the Shores of Silver Lake* by Laura Ingalls Wilder. I struggled to capture how that black pony's four legs gathered together underneath, airborne for a split second.

And I remember the three-hour drives north in June, from the time I was four until I was thirteen, to a campground on Michigan's Little Finger peninsula, where we'd live in a Winnebago all summer. I would look out the window and imagine myself on a galloping horse. Whenever we passed a horse in a pasture off the highway, I'd ask Dad to stop so I could pet it. He'd just laugh.

Even later, after I grew up, I'd ask. Even now, I ask. It's a running family joke. You cannot stop on the highway and pet every horse you see.

When I was ten, my mother had a friend who had horses. One day, the friend invited us for a ride. She put me on a pony named Dapples. I was sitting mounted when another horse strayed close to Dapples. He complained with a buck that tossed me to the ground on my butt.

My mom's friend put me on another pony, and we rode. I would have happily stayed with Dapples. He didn't frighten me. The fall didn't wound me. No matter that I sat on another pony's back; I'd returned to the saddle, and that meant I'd won.

That's my first memory of riding.

It never occurred to me to ask for lessons. Nobody I knew took lessons. I considered myself lucky to have one butt-bruising afternoon. From that day until my late twenties, I could count the number of times I rode a horse on one hand.

"Cries" are too weak a description for Maddy's glass-breaking screams, which, though they might not wake the dead, could and did wake the living. Trying to sleep on the couch in my mother's living room after family Christmases, I didn't understand the cause of Maddy's unhappiness. It seemed to me she had a great life. She had no job, no bills, and she had plenty of attention, food, clean diapers, and every toy known to humanity.

I didn't understand her development as a human being.

"She doesn't recognize me," I'd say to Mary.

"She's two and a half. She sees you once a year."

Maddy was becoming beautiful to look at: saucer eyes, plate-round face, platinum hair, movie star grin. But she was prickly to the touch. In fact, she refused most handling by anybody except her parents. Many people, strangers, were drawn to Maddy and invaded her evolving personal space, Mary said. The sensory overload disturbed her; best let her come to you, she advised. No problem. In nature, pretty things are often dangerous—like the poison arrow dart frog.

Brian and Mary had met Maddy's birth mother, a teen who knew she couldn't raise a child. They'd also met her birth grandmother, who described her daughter as a "handful." She said that if Maddy became anything like her mom, she'd keep Brian and Mary on their toes.

Our summer campground closed the year I turned thirteen. The following summer, I spent a few weeks with my dad's father in rural northern Michigan. Behind his home, a forest grew and trails led to a beach on Grand Traverse Bay.

One day, a young couple moved into the vacant stone bungalow next door. The woman, a distant cousin many times removed, brought with her Abby, the most beautiful horse I'd ever known—the most beautiful because I'd seen so few real horses.

My cousin indulged my excitement. She had grown up well-heeled in the Chicago area. As a child, she'd had a succession of her own horses and showed for years. Then she'd turned sixteen and jettisoned horses like old Barbie dolls. "I got interested in boys and cars." I'd nodded as though I understood her choice. Inside, I considered her a Judas who'd betrayed all girls who wished for horses and never had them.

Now, though, she could be forgiven. Now, she had Abby. More important, now she would share Abby—with me. She said I could groom Abby and give her treats every day. She might even give me lessons sometime.

I rode Abby once. We walked, bareback, down to the beach.

I left Grandpa's for a family outing for about a month. By the time I returned, the cousin and her husband had moved out. They'd sold Abby.

It happened without warning. Marble could have been the catalyst, or perhaps he was simply the first expression of something already inside Maddy, just waiting for the right moment.

Marble worked at the fairgrounds in Franken-muth, Michigan. He ferried children in a circle at four dollars a ride. Placed on top of his willing back, Maddy sat up and smiled wider than the sea. After that first ride, every time Brian and Mary took her to the fair, Maddy demanded time with Marble. He was, she believed, her horse. She was three.

"Maddy loves horses, just like you," Mary told me.

My conversations about Maddy changed from the decibel level of her screams to how soon I could ride with her.

Maddy already had the leggy body coveted by any classically trained equestrian. Her build, of course, must have come from her birth mother, who had another reason besides youth to give up her baby for adoption. She had her sights set on a career. At seventeen, she had an impressive resume showing saddlebreds.

"Did you know that Maddy loves horses?" I asked my dad. "Isn't that cool?"

He sniffed, unimpressed. "All little girls love horses."

My first boyfriend was allergic to horses but open-minded enough to consider giving me riding lessons as a Christmas gift. We broke up before December 25. I returned his house key but kept the idea. I had a job, money, a car, and no excuse not to learn how to ride. I was twenty-eight.

Jobs took me away from Michigan. In Tennessee, I rode trails, and I vacationed in Montana on a week-long cattle drive. In California, I discovered the rush of jumping over foot-high Xs. I returned to the Midwest, landing in Illinois, where I briefly leased a mountainous, 17-hand draft-cross named Goliath. He threw me off once when I asked for a canter. It was a long way down.

A few months later, my trainer sat me on a fine-featured Arabian she was selling for the owners. I'm 4 feet, 10 inches; the Arabian stood a petite 14.1 hands. We circled the arena a few times. She felt good, like a comfy boot.

Then a student came in and announced that the space shuttle Columbia had disintegrated over Texas. I was an editor and had to get to the newsroom right away. I dismounted and decided, right away: I bought the Arabian for $2,000. In my first official act as a first-time horse owner—at the age of thirty-seven—I changed her name from Katie to PageWon (pronounced "page one," a nod to my profession).

I looked forward to the day when Maddy would ride PageWon. It should have been easy. I lived in northern Illinois, Brian and Mary in the Detroit suburbs, and other family members in Chicago.

Two years later, Maddy still hadn't met my horse. I moved to Albuquerque, bringing PageWon with me. Maddy was five, old enough to travel and visit someday.

For eighteen months I suffered under New Mexico's unrelenting sun. It enervated me the way lack of sunshine unnerves victims of seasonal affective disorder. I had no job when I relocated to Chicago at age forty. My address, at first, was the basement in the home of my brother and sister-in-law, David and Erin. PageWon would not fit—literally, metaphorically, and financially.

That Christmas, Maddy overheard me discussing PageWon's fate. I spoke in the flippant way adults do when they don't want to pass their discomfort on to others.

"You're selling PageWon?" Maddy asked her aunt Judas.

She turned and walked away. She never did get to ride PageWon.

Weeks after I moved into the basement, Maddy called to invite me to her horse show. She'd been taking lessons on Morgans since she'd turned six the previous November. I had missed one show already and had to miss this one, too. But I would not miss the following one.

Maddy signed up to show in two classes that day. She and two other riders competed in the first event. Mary and I conspired like soccer moms as we eyed the competition, deeming one a threat and the other a nonfactor.

"She's at least in second place already," I whispered.

Then, approaching a corner, Maddy appeared to reach down for her stirrup. That's what it looked like to us, seated on the other end of the arena. We couldn't see that another rider's horse had come so close to Maddy's horse, BJ, that their heads actually brushed against each other briefly. BJ objected by tossing his head, throwing Maddy off balance in a revised version of what Dapples had done to me so many years ago. It wasn't so much a fall as a slip in slow motion. Regardless, she exited BJ's saddle.

Maddy's trainer and parents were at her side in seconds.

"Go back to your seats," the trainer told Brian and Mary. "She needs to focus."

He put her back on BJ. The audience clapped.

When they lined up at the end of the class, Maddy sat tall, looked straight ahead, and smiled.

The judge gave her one truth about riding—"Everybody falls"—and a third-place ribbon.

Later that night, I called Maddy into the guest room of their home before I went to bed. "Some people say you have to fall ten times before you are a real rider," I told her. "You're only six. I didn't even start riding until I was twenty-eight. You're already on your way. I'm proud of you."

Maddy walked out without saying a word. The next morning, I didn't mention her fall. Instead, I asked about her lessons. She said she would be there on Thursday.

I've wondered whether it truly is in all little girls' nature to love horses. I've seen girls the same age as Maddy yell in fear when they're put eye to eye with a 1,000-pound Goliath. I've seen girls who treat lessons so frivolously that they arrive without their boots. Would a boy show up to football practice without his helmet? I've seen their love of horses leave as years go by.

Because Maddy's story is just beginning, I cannot know how it will end. For now, she and I are both like the horse on the cover of *By the Shores of Silver Lake*, galloping unreservedly, its four legs meeting under its belly, suspended in air and time.

Melissa Birks

Contributors

Glenda C. Beall ("An Angel Called Amos") lives in Hayesville, North Carolina, with husband, Barry, and their dog, Rocky. She writes for local newspapers, teaches seniors to write their life stories, leads the North Carolina Writers' Network West, and facilitates poetry readings. Her poetry and essays have appeared in numerous magazines and journals.

C. L. Beck ("Horse on Lap"), a freelance writer and photographer, lives in Utah with her husband, Russ, and their dog, Corky Porky Pie. Her penchant for writing stems from a love of reading, and she credits her parents, Robert and Roberta Kieliger, for supplying her with a constant stream of good books when she was a child.

Melissa Birks ("All Little Girls Love Horses") now lives in her own apartment in Chicago, where she works as a freelance journalist and attends graduate school. Maddy continues to take riding lessons, as of this writing. PageWon lives with a nice woman in Taos, New Mexico.

Ina Mae Brooks ("Crossing Over") is a freelance writer who works from her Lamar, Missouri, home. She is a retired social worker, disability rights advocate, and mentor for first-grade children. She and her husband of fifty-six years have four children, six grandchildren, and three great-grandchildren.

Lesa Cameron ("Rebel with a Cause") lives with her husband and two children in Greenwood, Nebraska. Since giving up the position of library director to pursue her dream of being a freelance writer, she has had several articles and short stories published. She is currently working with an agent to publish her first novel.

Ruth Cardello ("That's Love") is a kindergarten teacher who lives on a small farm in Northern Rhode Island with her husband, two stepchildren, and three horses. If there is a happier place on Earth, she cannot imagine it.

Jean R. Clark ("My Trail Guardian") retired as director of special education in a suburb of Phoenix, Arizona. After her retirement, she and her husband moved to Camp Verde, Arizona. For eleven years, she rode her horses on area trails and wrote feature stories for Verde Valley Newspapers, Inc. Now a widow, she lives in Las Cruces, New Mexico.

Sally Clark ("A Love Affair to Remember") and the boy she met at the stable, Mike, have been married lovers since 1970. They enjoy living in Fredericksburg, Texas, with their children and grandchildren. She began writing after they retired from the restaurant business. Since then, she has published children's stories, poetry, greeting cards, humor, and creative nonfiction.

Cheryl Dale ("When Shawna Met Sonny") is the mother of three children and lives in Yakima, Washington, with her husband. She grew up with horses, and her children began riding as soon as they were old enough to hold the reins. A human resources director, she is also a writing, quilting, and Harley Davidson motorcycle enthusiast.

Traci Durrell-Khalife ("Four Legs, Two Wheels, One Wish") has owned and shown horses since childhood and has been judging horse shows since 1980. She also has a passion for model horses and organizes an annual model competition in Corvallis, Oregon, where she resides. She has written numerous magazine articles on the model horse hobby. Traci is employed at Oregon State University.

Lauren C. Esping ("A Forelock to Lean On") lives in Indiana, where she rides and trains her twelve-year-old Warmblood gelding, Dino. She is currently a sophomore in college, majoring in pre-physical therapy, with the dream to one day open a therapeutic riding center and work her beloved Dino into the therapy program.

Gayle Farmer ("A Pet Theory") loves horses, as anyone who's ever known her will tell you. She has devoted her life to hunting, showing, breeding, and training hunters and jumpers. She lives with her husband, Jeff, in Palm Springs, California, where she writes young adult horse novels loosely based on her real-life experiences.

Mary Forseth ("Trinity") resides in Northern Minnesota with her husband, two sons, and an assortment of domestic critters. Her career experience thus far includes freelance illustrator, retail manager, full-time mom, and currently, educational paraprofessional and search-and-rescue volunteer. Her goal is to continue developing her writing and illustration skills and to venture into children's literature.

Elizabeth King Gerlach ("A Man's Best Friend") grew up riding horses at her grandparent's farm in east Texas. A writer living in Oregon, she is the author of *Just This Side of Normal: Glimpses Into Life with Autism* and *Autism Treatment Guide* (Future Horizons.)

Nancy L. Gillen ("I Dreamt of Horses") was born in Rochester, New York, and currently resides in the Finger Lakes region of western New York. She has been married to her husband, Kip, for thirty years. In 1995, she got her first miniature horse and established a small hobby farm, Dare to Dream Miniatures.

Charlotte Godfrey ("A Horse-Shopping Adventure") rode her grandfather's mule, jumping over small bushes, using a halter and a lead rope as a bridle and a burlap bag as a saddle. Eventually, her grandfather bought her a horse, who turned out to be a terrorist with hooves, but that is another story. She has owned and operated a boarding stable in Michigan since 1989.

Maureen Gould ("More Than a Horse, of Course") lives in Stanwood, Washington, with her horses. She is a natural barefoot trimmer and the founder of For the Horse Equine Rescue (*www.forthehorse.net*).

Terri Hardison ("Mooney and Me") lives in Fresno, California, and works as a teacher's aid in a special education class for preschoolers with autism. Horses are her number-one passion, and she enjoys riding them as often as she can.

Betsy O'Brien Harrison ("A Graceful Exit") is a happily married, Pittsburgh, Pennsylvania-based freelance writer. She has been a horse-show mom for more than ten years, and she is an advocate for Alzheimer's caregiver support, due to her current role as primary caregiver for her mom. Her work has appeared in various national publications, including *A Cup of Comfort® for Sisters*.

John C. Hobson ("Mrs. Bladic's Mare") was born in Lizmore, County Waterford, Ireland. He was an elementary school teacher for thirty-two years. Now retired, he pursues his lifelong association with horses as a trainer and ferrier on his farm in Southern Ontario, Canada. He shares his life with his wife, Jeannette Vroom, their Jack Russell terriers, Trina and Ellie, and several cats.

Loraine J. Hudson ("The Starting Line") lives with her husband and daughter in Eagle, Michigan. She works full-time at Michigan State University and writes children's chapter books under the pen name of Judith Wade—that is, when she and Silver Blur aren't out riding.

Cheri Jalbert ("Bummer and Gypsy") lives in the mountains of Maine on a farm with her husband. Together they have one son, several foster children, five Great Danes, ten cats, two horses, and one grandma who keeps them all out of trouble. Retired from emergency medicine, she loves to write about her experiences.

Jim Johnson ("Clyde-Cross'd Romance") lives in northern Virginia with his wife, four cats, and a cookie-loving chestnut mare. When he's not doling out treats to the menagerie or working for a government contractor, he writes short stories and novels in the genres of science fiction, fantasy, historical fiction, and whatever else his muse whispers in his ear.

Juliet Johnson ("At Clyde's Pace") is a full-time mom and part-time carriage driver in Los Angeles. She's been published in *The Imperfect Parent, Los Angeles Family Magazine,* and *A Cup of Comfort*® *for Mothers-to-Be,* among others. Along with the wondrous Clyde, she is inspired daily by her magical family: Barry, Bruce, Nathan, Emma, Lilly, and Gramma Bonnie.

Robyn Keeney ("The Backyard Race") is a full-time news producer and horse addict. She lives in Atlanta, Georgia, with her dog, Zoe, and the dream of someday owning a horse of her own. When she's not in the saddle, she enjoys reading, traveling, and taking random dance classes.

Marilyn Dorothea King ("Fagan's Gifts") lives in Western Australia with her husband, Howard. At fifty-seven, she is an accomplished performance poet and writer. Her skills as a poet laureate are in great demand at conferences and other events, and in the guise of the "Mad Poet," she uses comedy to help audiences release *their* inner poets.

Gary B. Luerding ("Of Cowboys and Courage") is a retired army sergeant and high school administrator. He lives in Southern Oregon with his wife of forty-four years. They have three children and eight grandchildren.

Libby McKay, DVM, ("Freeing Feetsy") has been in private practice for twenty years. She lives near Lexington, South Carolina, on six acres she shares with an assortment of four-legged "kids." Her passions are her work and riding (dressage). Other interests include reading, writing, landscaping, studying Scottish history, and dreaming up new renovation projects for her 120-year-old cottage.

Heather Mitchell ("My Chocolate-Coated Destiny") was raised in the woodlands of Northern Ontario, Canada, and as an adult turned both her pen and paintbrushes to the rugged countryside around her and the creatures she encountered there. She is an award-winning poet, equine photographer, artist, and avid horsewoman.

Ishbel Moore ("My $1 Lifesaver"), originally from Scotland, lives in Winnipeg, Manitoba, Canada, where she is a medical transcriptionist. Her lifelong dream of having horses finally came true in 2003 with the gift of a white Arabian mare called Promise. Her love of horses and writing combined when she began writing for *Horse Country Magazine*. She is also the author of several published young adult novels.

Amy Ammons Mullis ("A Sensational Contract") works as a church secretary in a town the size of a pony's nose in upstate South Carolina. Her muses are a bottle of cold grape soda and a sister who never gives up. Look for more of her work in *A Cup of Comfort® for Writers*.

Sheina North ("King of My Heart") has two completed fantasy novels and a third is in progress. She also writes nonfiction and poetry. By day, she is a technical writer and Web designer, and she has been honored with an Award of Excellence from the Society of Technical Communication. She lives with her family (human and canine) in Albuquerque, New Mexico.

Denise J. Pullis ("Mercy's Magic") has been involved with riding, showing, breeding, and training horses since the age of five. She lives with her husband, Tim, sons Andrew and Benjamin, two dogs, two cats, and six horses on Silversong Farm in upstate New York. Her work has appeared in *EQUUS* and *Miniature Horse Voice* magazines and in *Straight from the Heart II*.

Graham E. Rogers ("Attached") lives in Fordingbridge in the United Kingdom. He was born in the East End of London just before the end of World War II. After a youth spent playing on bombsites, he left London, and following a variety of careers, he is now a storyteller, working mainly with school-aged children.

Pam Karlsgodt Roylance ("Track Tales") has been an Arabian breeder for more than thirty years and became a licensed race trainer in 1986. Two Arabians that she bred, trained, and still owns and one client's horse that she trained all received Darley Award nominations. A graduate of Montana State University and a part-time freelance journalist, she resides on her horse farm in southwest Idaho near Homedale.

Nancy Schaufele ("The Pony Farm") was born in Atlanta, Georgia, and now lives in Colorado near Mesa Verde National Park, where she spends her time hiking and horseback riding in Four Corners. Now retired, she had a long and satisfying career as a counselor, specializing in post-traumatic stress, and she co-owned and directed a national employee-assistance program. She and her husband share four children, two grandchildren, two large dogs, one cat, and two horses.

Rebekah Schow ("Heartland") lives in the western United States, where she enjoys the convenience of city living and the fun of ATV exploration in the nearby mountains. She is a freelance writer and an avid photographer and holds a master's degree in mental health counseling, but she considers her life as a full-time homemaker to be her most challenging and rewarding endeavor.

Rena Sherwood ("Riding Blind") has lived both homeless in England and homed in America, and she now resides in the Philadelphia area. A freelance writer, she has published numerous stories and poems in magazines and e-zines, such as *Atomjack*, *StoryStation*, and *GlassFire*. She hopes to be a white horse when she grows up.

Deanna Stollar ("The Rescue Boat") resides with her husband, Terry, and their four children in Springfield, Oregon. A lecturer, Christian home educator, and freelance writer, she is the author of *It Takes a Parent: A Teaching Guide for the First Time Parent/Coach* and coauthor of *Coaching Policy Debate: Transitioning from a Debate Class to a Debate Club*.

Christine K. Thomas ("Too Precious to Waste") lives in Middleburg, Virginia, along with her Paint, Avery; her mare, Mrs. Weasley; and abundant cats and dogs. She is employed as a veterinary technician at a local small animal emergency service, hence the abundance of cats and dogs. She has ridden horses for almost thirty-five years and has loved them a great deal longer.

Ellen Tomaszewski ("Back in the Saddle with Sundance") lives with her husband in southeastern Washington state, where she writes full time. This story was adapted from her recently finished memoir, *My Blindy Girl*, which describes the struggles and accomplishments resulting from Katy's rare visual impairment, achromatopsia. Katy recently graduated from college, and she still loves horses.

Susan B. Townsend ("The Reunion") is the author of *A Bouquet for Mom* and *A Bouquet for Grandmother* and co-editor of *A Cup of Comfort® Book of Prayer*. She lives in southeastern Virginia on a farm with her husband, five children, and a menagerie of animals, including a pony named Angel.

Sarah Underwood ("The Color of Honey and Just as Sweet") is a University of Lethbridge student who plans to enter the field of animal behavior, likely in horse training and sales. You will most often find her horseback riding, taking photographs, and frequently doing both at the same time. She has recently started her own photography company, specializing in equine subject matter.

Edward Varno ("A Birthday Story") lives in Canandaigua, New York, and writes under the pen name of Ben Theyre. He has written for various publications over the years but is best known for his horse philosophy column, "Life Lessons on the Trail," featured in *The Trail Rider Magazine*, a national publication.

Samantha Ducloux Waltz ("Mirror, Mirror in the Stall") is a freelance writer in Portland, Oregon. Her essays can be seen in the *Cup of Comfort*® series, the *Chicken Soup* series, and other anthologies, including *Horse Crazy* and *The Healing Touch of Horses*. She has also published adult nonfiction and juvenile fiction under the names Samantha Ducloux and Samellyn Wood.

Wanda West ("Run Like the Wind") lives on a small farm in Bruce, Mississippi, where she raises Arabian and quarter horses. She enjoys her career in travel nursing, but she is always glad to get home to her horses, dogs, and cats. She writes stories as a way to record and share her many wonderful experiences with all her critters.

About the Editor

Colleen Sell has compiled more than twenty volumes of the *Cup of Comfort*® book series. A veteran writer and editor, she has authored, ghost-written, or edited more than a hundred books; published scores of magazine articles and essays; and served as editor-in-chief of two award-winning magazines, associate editor of a national business magazine, and home and garden columnist of a regional newsmagazine. She and the love of her midlife, T. N. Trudeau, share a pioneer farmhouse on a future lavender farm in the Pacific Northwest.